CALLING

CALLING

A Song for the Baptized

Caroline A. Westerhoff

COWLEY PUBLICATIONS
Cambridge ✦ Boston
Massachusetts

Library of Congress Cataloging-in-Publication Data:
  Westerhoff, Caroline A., 1940 -
  Calling: a song for the baptized / Caroline A. Westerhoff.
      p.   cm.
  ISBN 1-56101-101-0 (alk. paper)
  1. Baptism. 2. Christian life—Anglican authors. I. Title.
BV811.2.W4   1994   94-27023
234'.161—dc20   CIP

"The Sea" was previously published as "The Gift of Power" in *Liturgy*, Volume 6, Number 2 (1986). © The Liturgical Conference, 8750 Georgia Avenue, Suite 123, Silver Spring, Maryland 20912. All rights reserved. Used with permission.

Quotations from the *Book of Common Prayer* of the Episcopal Church are all drawn from the baptismal service, pages 299 to 310. Biblical quotations are from the *New Revised Standard Version*.

Cover photograph by Fred Whitehead. Cover design by Vicki Black.

Calling was edited by Cynthia Shattuck and typeset by Vicki Black.

This book is printed on recycled, acid-free paper and was produced in the United States of America.

Cowley Publications
28 Temple Place
Boston, Massachusetts 02111

For John and Nanno

Table of Contents

Foreword

MY WIFE CAROLINE AND I have worked together for nearly two decades and during that time we have co-authored two books—*On the Threshold of God's Future* and *Living Into Our Baptism*—a significant accomplishment in itself! For the past three years I have been encouraging her to write her own book. And now she has done so, and I am delighted with the result.

Caroline has always been an extremely gifted consultant, process enabler, teacher, and administrator. She has served as a principal of an Episcopal Day School, a senior consultant with the Alban Institute, a visiting lecturer at the School of Theology at Sewanee. She is now the Canon Educator of the Episcopal Diocese of Atlanta, a licensed lay preacher, and a conference leader for the College of Preachers. But Caroline's needle—too often hidden in the proverbial haystack—is the depth of her knowledge and theological acumen. Perhaps that is because her mode of communication is in the realm of the "theopoetic," to quote Amos Wilder, the New Testament scholar and poet. I am by temperament a speculative intellectual type, though I have always imagined myself to be an affective intuitive one. It was only after I met Caroline that I really knew who I was and why we complemented each other so well; she had the temperament I desired.

While never anti-intellectual, Anglicans are more at home with the intuitive way of thinking and knowing than the intellectual. They prefer art to philosophy and are more comfortable in the world of symbol, myth, and ritual than that of systematic theology. They are more at home with liturgy that makes use of the arts rather than discursive prose, because Anglicans affirm the anagogical, the metaphorical, the paradoxical, and the symbolic in the exploration of human experience. That is why some of their best theologians have been poets. Recognizing that human nature and society are more deeply motivated by images and fables than ideas and concepts, Anglicans are apt to emphasize the imagination, endeavoring to hold objectivity and subjectivity in tension. And this, I have learned, is how Caroline thinks and writes.

In an insightful lecture on preaching, David Buttrick remarked that most sermons, like eighteenth-century paintings, are delivered in a third-person, objective, descriptive style. But people nowadays no longer think in a third-person, objective fashion: they think "perspectively," in structured movements of thought. For a long time preachers have unpacked the Scriptures from an historical-critical perspective, but now they may need to return to a search for metaphors, allegories, and images to make biblical faith intelligible to contemporary people.

Caroline approaches the Scriptures from a dialogical, conversational, narrative perspective and engages our prophetic imaginations—to use Walter Brueggeman's phrase. She knows how to communicate by keeping the "I" and the "Eye" of the communicator in creative tension. In this book she develops strong characters and writes poetically to convey profound theory and faithful theology.

In the early church it took as long as three years to prepare for baptism. Along the way the catechumens were tested, and only when the community discerned they were ready did they enter a final period of spiritual activity, followed by an elaborate baptismal rite and fifty days of enlightenment. While this tradition is returning with the rite of Christian initiation of adults, most baptisms today are still conducted with very little preparation. Most people do not even remember or celebrate the day. Instead, our focus is on ordination. People go to seminary for three years of preparation, pass through an elaborate testing program, celebrate an elaborate ordination rite, and remember and celebrate their ordination days. Is it any wonder that the ministry of the laity is not taken seriously?

Ministry means service: service to the *magister*, to God. We are all enrolled in and empowered for that ministry at our baptism. At baptism we are incorporated into Christ's body, infused with Christ's character, and empowered to be Christ's presence in the world. Ministry is not something in particular that we do; it is what we are about in everything we do. This book is about how we are to understand daily life and work as ministry, how we are to live in the world as a baptized people.

While I am aware of a host of fine books on the ministry of the baptized, I find *Calling* the most original and profound. Caroline understands the deep meaning and implications of baptism. As a lay person in the church she has exerted her power and authority accordingly, and through the years she has aided other lay persons to do the same. Once trained as a biologist, she brings a unique understanding of the organic nature of human systems to her work. Her love of the natural order shows clearly. As a gifted poet she brings a new imaginative perspective to her theory and her theology. As a lay practitioner she communicates wise insights and implications for the Christian life of faith.

This book has many uses, and in my guide for study included at the back I have offered a number of suggestions for ways of incorporating its insights both as individuals and as members of the body of Christ. Now that I have read *Calling* three times, I know that I intend to read it again. I also intend to recommend it in my teaching and more than likely quote it in my writing, for it can be a beautiful delight to use a spouse's work in your own.

— John H. Westerhoff
Associate Rector,
Director of the Institute of Pastoral Studies,
St. Luke's Episcopal Church, Atlanta, Georgia

Acknowledgments

IN 1980 FRANK K. ALLAN, then rector of St. Anne's Episcopal Church in Atlanta, invited me into the pulpit one Sunday morning in June. I had the termerity to accept his invitation (or perhaps his challenge), and so with the formidable act of preaching I began the process of discovering my theological voice—at least in a more intentional way than before. For the record, he is now the Right Reverend Frank K. Allan, Bishop of Atlanta, and I serve as a canon on his staff. I am grateful for his continuing confidence and support.

Many people have contributed to this voice-finding over the years, but four groups particularly come to mind: members of St. Anne's and St. Bartholomew's parishes in Atlanta and of St. Clement's in Canton, Georgia, whose pulpits have been open and weloming to a lay preacher; and members of the Episcopal Church Women all over the country who encouraged me as I tested my ideas and my words in the six years I served as consultant to their national board. I am grateful for their energetic engagement.

The staff at Cowley Publications have been nothing less than superb. The editorial director, Cynthia Shattuck, has guided me with a mixture of firmness, appreciation, good humor, and warmth. I am grateful for her keen commitment to clarity and precision, which she manages to couple with flexibility and respect for the writer's voice. And it was Vicki Black, Cowley's managing editor, who came up with a basic organization for the manuscript that headed us in the way we would go. I am grateful for her imagination and her artistic sense.

Finally, I am grateful to John Westerhoff, my long-time colleague and toughest critic, for demonstrating to me that love and agreement are not the same thing. He has always been willing to tell me the truth—pro and con—about my work. One cannot hope to find her voice without such friends in her life.

Introduction

I WAS BAPTIZED ON THE AFTERNOON of April 6, 1947, in the chapel of Glenn Memorial Methodist Church in Atlanta, Georgia. My younger brother Benjamin was baptized at the same time. My grandmother and a family friend signed the certificates as witnesses. It was Easter Day—one day short of my seventh birthday. I wore a pink dress trimmed in white lace and my first corsage— pink carnations and baby's-breath—was pinned to the shoulder. This book reflects my struggles over the ensuing forty-seven years to come to terms with all the implications of that event.

I have long heard it said that baptism is the primary sacrament ordaining us for ministry as disciples of Jesus. However, I worship and work in a church that remains highly clericalized—all our good words and intentions to the contrary. As I have helped others look at questions of call and vocation, I have entertained questions about the form of my own. Over time it has become clear to me that the lay order is my home. It has become my passion to explore the life of the baptized and to ask questions about the nature of the ministry we are to undertake. I have long been licensed to preach and delight in doing so, and I now find myself a canon of the church. Yet the pew is where I am mostly called to be, engaged in the strenuous work of worship.

This collection of reflections and meditations on baptism emerges from my explorations, and it begins in an unexpected place: the realm of the imagination. I have always been deeply touched by the words and paintings and songs of those who saw and heard beyond my senses, and I have instinctively started with that which I could imagine. But it was Amos Wilder, the distinguished biblical scholar and poet, who gave me confidence in my ways. He writes:

> Imagination is a necessary component of all profound knowing and celebration; all remembering, realizing, and anticipating; all faith, hope, and love. When imagination fails doctrines become ossified, witness and proclamation wooden, doxologies and litanies empty, consolations hollow, and ethics legalistic.... Then that which once gave life begins to lull and finally to suffocate us.[1]

It was the strength and the warning of Wilder's words that inspired the underlying form of this book—a departure from the discursive, the rationalistic, the prosaic.

Early on I became aware of the recurrence of certain themes in the Christian life: the compelling implications of the cross, the power of suffering love, the future that finally belongs to God, our inevitable connections with each other. The image of a variety of melodies weaving around these themes began to take shape for me, and, with the encouragement of friends more musical than I and the help of my editors, the format for this "song for the baptized" emerged, complete with a prelude, movements, themes, variations, and a finale.

I invite you now to enter with me the symbolic and poetic way—the way of the child. It is the first and truest path toward the power of our rebirth in baptism. I invite you to undertake the rich but difficult work of

---

1 Amos Niven Wilder, *Theopoetic: Theology and the Religious Imagination* (Philadelphia: Fortress Press, 1976), 2.

this imaginative realm with me, for I believe it to be work of necessity, not a pastime of luxury. It is the labor of urgency for which we too often do not take time—to our peril. If the eyes and ears of our imaginations can only remain open and clear, we will perceive the fresh messages of touch which God is ever presenting to us.

PRELUDE

Calling

---- There is one hope in God's call to us. ----

I VISITED MY GRANDMOTHER in rural South Georgia every summer when I was of grade-school age. My family lived in New York State at the time, and my parents saw this respite from "Yankee influence" as opportunity for me to know and to claim my heritage as a child of the South, a time for the red Georgia clay to color my clothes and my heart.

Calling was what we did in the afternoon. Sometimes Nanno and I would freshen up and go to call on others. (A starched dress was a must.) More often than not Nanno's friends came to call on us. They just appeared at the door, smelling of lilac and powder, an unspoken invitation delivered and received.

We sat in the tall green wicker rockers on my grandmother's front screened porch and sipped icy glasses of mint tea and ate her acclaimed sunshine cake. The women talked of weather and crops and lamented the lint in the air from the cotton gin. They talked about who was sick; who was spatting with whom; who was marrying whom; who was divorcing whom; who was expecting; who was dying. I rocked and listened and heard more than they ever knew. (A lot goes on in a small town in the heat of summer!)

Even then all the talk was not palatable to me. To my morally superior ears these good Methodist ladies seemed to relish the tragic and the seamy. But even then

I sensed that involvement did not stop with the telling. I sensed that prayers were offered in the midst of chatter and tea and cake, prayers that later would be offered anew in kitchens and bedrooms; that calls would be made to the newborn, the sick, the dying, the frightened—even if they were unfortunate enough to have the wrong color skin. (Prejudice also sat in those wicker chairs.) Cakes would be baked and meals served because these women had come to call.

Why did these women gather day after day? Habit? That certainly was part of it. They gathered in the afternoon because they had *always* gathered in the afternoon. Habits are patterns of mind and heart developed through continuing practice over time—whether the practice is by intention or not. There is nothing wrong with habits as long as they bring refreshment to who we are and what we do. Habits have power for good and for ill; habits liberate, and habits bind.

Habits release us from obligation to think through every move we make. Responding out of habit means we can do two things at once. Our imaginations can be free to run down the street while our eyes look both ways at the crossing. And when the lights go out and the room becomes dark as pitch, we can move around familiar obstacles and find the path to the door.

There is another side to habits, however. Because they are automatic acts, we tend not to scrutinize them, not to turn them over and look underneath the comfort of their repetition. We do not ask how we are using them to avoid, how they might be causing harm to ourselves or to others, how they might be resulting in stagnation. We sit on the porch in the afternoon, eat our cake, drink our tea, and isolate ourselves from what might call us to break molds of security and convenience and move into the unfamiliar and cloudy, to risk receiving or fashioning something new.

As Christians we have heard and accepted the call into the grand and precarious quest of discipleship, and as disciples we are to become bold callers. The call has to do with forming habits—holy habits that direct us out of ourselves toward others and the Other. Habits that polish away the grit and grime we accumulate so readily. Habits that smooth the rough places that snag and tear. Habits that wash the imagination in fresh possibility. Habits that straighten the spine and strengthen the heart. Habits that feed us and bring us cheer.

> *The children in our midst look around and ask (as those children always will): "What are we to do if we are followers of Jesus? What habits do we practice?"*

Let's return to my grandmother's porch and the green wicker rockers and the good Methodist ladies. They gathered out of habit, and they gathered to rock in each other's company.

While it is true that moments of deep and wrenching truth may only come as we, like Jacob, wrestle with the spirits on a solitary bank of a river in the night, we are to test those wrestlings around the fire of community. We are created to be unique, unlike any other who was or will be. Yet we are also created to live with each other—to eat and drink together, to hold each other when we are afraid, to laugh together at our antics, to prod each other, and to forgive. It is in community that we can bear the pain of the limp we share with the wrestling Jacob. It is through the relational that we bear the tension of solitude.

I talked to a friend as he was emerging from the long valley of the shadow that follows the loss of relationship. In his case the bleakness was exacerbated by his work's requirement that he be on the road, in strange places with strangers, often eating alone. When he did return to his apartment in his own city, he found himself alone again. Human connections were dry; no one called for dinner because he had not been there when they had called before.

He described awakening one early morning during that dark and motionless span when heaven and earth catch their breaths and the terrors emerge. "If I were to die now in this bed," he realized, "no one would know for days." He then wept trembling tears as he heard for himself God's ancient words to Adam:

"It is not good that you should be alone. I have made helpers and partners for you. It is up to you to be in their company. You must reconnect with friends neglected. You must find chairs left empty in your absence. You must sit on porches and rock and chat, accepting the gifts of tea and cake that will relieve your gnawing need. You must give back the gift of your presence."

As Christians we are to receive callers and to be callers as well. We are to provide settings in which calling is anticipated and fostered. We are to leave our chairs and go to other porches, for there are many houses in the town and we never know where God will next come to call.

The children in our midst look around and ask (as those children always will): "Can we join the followers of Jesus, or are we to be alone? Will they let us lean against them when the way becomes hard? Will they lean against us?"

We return again to my grandmother's porch and the green wicker rockers and the good Methodist ladies.

They gathered out of habit. They gathered to rock in each other's company. They gathered to tell stories.

I heard of my great-grandfather, the drummer: he and a driver sold hats from the back of a motor car in South Carolina. I heard how my grandmother, his daughter, met my grandfather, the doctor, on a tennis court in the early years of this century. I heard how she walked up to the First Methodist Church and shot her revolver in the air to herald the end of the First World War and the return of her husband. I heard about Grandfather's medical practice among the poor—black and white—of rural Georgia, with my mother, the tomboy child, making rounds with him. I heard of his early death. I heard how Grandmother went back to school and resumed her calling as a teacher to support herself and her two young daughters.

I learned of my heritage, the frailty and fortitude of those who had come before me. I learned about the stuff from which I had sprung. From those stories I gathered life-clues—clues about celebration and the giving of gifts, about carrying on when the road gives out in front of you, about knowing what matters. I became clearer about who I was and who I could be as I rocked and sipped, crumbs spilling down the front of my starched dress.

I also heard stories about the other families represented in the green wicker circle. Even then I sensed that we were writing a larger and more complete history as we wove our particular ones together. The gathered ladies told about all kinds of people doing all kinds of things in all kinds of situations. I laughed; I shook my head; I wrinkled my nose; I tried hard not to cry. I saw that their stories were both similar to and different from mine. I began to sense that, while I was related to these others, I was not the same. I was someone with a story all her own. (How lives can be shaped in the heat of a South Georgia summer on a screened porch as good Methodist ladies spin their tales!)

But there was more. Certain phrases peppered the ladies' stories which, as I became aware of them, opened up another dimension of their accounts. "By the grace of God," was a recurring one. "Thank the Lord," was another. And, "God give them strength," or "God give *me* strength." The murmurings were not casual; they were intentional. This God was someone the women knew and trusted.

God. I knew the name, of course, from Sunday school classes at the First Methodist Church. I had heard Bible stories about people who talked to God, but they were long-ago people who wore funny costumes and did strange things. Then over time I began to weave a web of connections—ones I continue to make today—among the First Methodist Church and the porch and the town; among the characters in the Bible stories and the characters in the stories of our families; among the past, present, and future. The common thread seemed to be this God who was part of our rocking and talking and drinking and eating and yet who was also beyond them, over them. (I wondered if I should draw up an extra chair.)

To be human is to tell stories. We Christians are called to tell stories that are infused and alive with the presence of God so that we and the children in our midst can make connections. We are to be hearers, tellers, and bearers of story—tasks that require courage, imagination, and the ability to be quiet.

It is a fearsome thing to speak or write words that symbolize the essence of one's life. But if we do not, we cannot participate in the weaving of God's designs. It is a fearsome thing to speak or write words of other lives.

But if we do not dare, figures of the past and the present will be lost to children of the future. And we are to evoke the stories of those who have come to call. If we do not, they will go away, and chairs will be empty. We are to listen to stories being shouted in streets and whispered in corners. If we do not, we will miss the word of God.

> *The children in our midst look around and ask (as those children always will): "Where will we hear stories—all kinds of stories? You won't skip any of the pages, will you? May we sit in your lap and tell our stories, too?"*

My grandmother and her friends gathered because they had long practiced the art of gathering. Gathering is what they did on a summer's afternoon. They came together to be together, to share one another's company. And they flew kites of words into the still air. There may have been additional reasons, but for now a new question comes to mind: Why *Grandmother's* porch? While she had her shortcomings, there must have been something about Nanno's character that drew others into her presence.

From her I learned of the love of God. I always knew she loved me, no matter what I said or did. How did I know? What did I learn about my relationship with God and thus how I am to be with others? Some things defy analysis; however, I have intimations.

First, she never saw a contradiction between accepting me and demanding my best. Love did not mean anything goes; love meant setting and insisting on standards. But when I did not or could not meet them, love meant continuing presence. She called me beyond where I was in the moment to an expanded vision, and she walked with me along the way. She paused and extended a hand of balance when my steps faltered, and I believe she must have done the same as a teacher with her high school students. A diminutive woman, she was renowned for managing discipline in difficult situations. But it takes a really hardened character to resist the attention of one who does not give up, who does not go away; of one who pursues but who also moves ahead, calling out your name.

We are called to demand and to accept and then to demand again. Holding each other accountable is integral to caring.

Second, Nanno was hospitable, welcoming. The chairs on her porch were arranged in an inviting circle. They were green and freshly painted. The tea was cold. The cake was sweet and moist. Her dress was clean. She was ready to receive callers. And she always seemed to have time—for me and the Methodist ladies, for the ring of the telephone and the knock on the door. She seemed to know that callings would occur, that she would be interrupted.

We are called to arrange inviting spaces. We are called to stand at open doors and extend our hands. We are to be accessible, to make time, and to listen. We are to provide tea and cake. We are to be open to interruption.

Third, Nanno was immersed in the world around her. She loved to dig in the earth. She kept a large birdbath filled and carried on lively conversations with the regulars, fiercely scolding blue jay and squirrel for their rude intrusions. She read voraciously and passed on to me a love of the written word, especially that of the poet. She served as a substitute teacher in the high school well into her eighties. She crocheted edges of endless linen napkins and baby blankets, gifts of her own hands for all occasions. She lived in relationship—even to the characters of her beloved soap operas whom she befriended in her later years. She was extraordinary in her ordinariness.

We are called to see ourselves in connection with all things and all others. We are to know that what we say and do has implications beyond what we can perceive at the time—for good and for ill.

Fourth, Nanno was immersed in the community of faith. The First Methodist Church occupied a central position in her life. It was her primary community, and she was there every Sunday in her usual seat, greeting and singing and praying and nodding. She gave her money and her time and her heart. She read and knew her Bible, and her counsel was frequently sprinkled with familiar verses from the psalms. She knew beyond all shadow of a doubt that the Lord was her shepherd, and she daily walked in that confidence. She would have made no clear distinction between her life in the church and her life on the porch and in the larger community— she moved so naturally among them.

We are called to ground our lives in the worship of God. We are to seek community and guidance in God's church and are to carry the gospel of reconciliation into all places. But the divine dwelling is not limited by our designs, so we are called to look for God's activity in likely and unlikely situations, and we are to bring word of this activity back to the church for *its* invigoration as well.

Fifth, she was able to tolerate ambiguity. Life did not settle out facilely in hues of black and white. She had raised children. She had buried a husband. She had known plenty, and she had worried about getting by. She had worked in the system known as school—not unlike the system known as church. She loved her friends; she had known their betrayal. She was able to see life in the blending shades of gray necessary to keep sanity and integrity intact.

We are called to live with questions, to appreciate the question mark as punctuating faith. We are to know that we do not know. We are to depend on others for their part of God's truth.

Finally, she had a sense of humor. She could tell stories on herself; she could hold matters in perspective. One of her favorite sayings was, "This too shall pass." It kept her going when life seemed to throw one obstacle after another under her feet. I try to remember to say it as well. Her final act on this earth was to tease me lovingly and then chuckle as she died.

We are called to laugh.

The porch on which we sat all those long summers ago faced River Street. In front of the porch grew a large ginkgo tree. Grandfather had ordered it for Grandmother. There was no other tree like it in town, and it blazed with gold November fire the day we buried her. I carried a leaf from that ginkgo tree in my jacket pocket from the house to the First Methodist Church and then to the graveyard, and we sang "Amazing Grace."

First Movement

BAPTISM AND MINISTRY

We thank you, Father, for the water of Baptism.
In it we are buried with Christ in his death.
By it we share in his resurrection.
Through it we are reborn by the Holy Spirit.
Therefore in joyful obedience to your Son,
we bring into his fellowship
those who come to him in faith,
baptizing them in the Name of the Father,
and of the Son, and of the Holy Spirit.

Holy Habits

---- Will you continue in the apostles' teaching and fellowship, in the breaking of bread, and in the prayers? ----

THE CHILDREN IN OUR MIDST look around and ask (as those children always will): "What are we to do if we are followers of Jesus? What habits do we practice?" Another way of phrasing the question might be: "What defines these followers in the first place?"

One source of answers is the prayer book catechism. Here we read that the ministers in the eucharistic community are those who are to carry out its mission of reconciliation and restoration, of reuniting the fractured peoples of the earth with each other and with God. These ministers are the church's laity, bishops, priests, and deacons, and to each is given a particular charge. So we begin with a presupposition: that each of the four orders of ministers has different functions to perform for the church, the body of Christ, and each is dependent upon the others to make up the whole. To say it another way, each order is a symbol for the others of what they are and what they are to be. A body is not in vigorous health when essential parts are missing.

In considering the ministry of the baptized within the eucharistic community, it is useful to think of a round table with four chairs drawn up for a meal or a serious talk. If any seat is missing or empty, the company is diminished, incomplete. Certain acts will not happen; certain words will not be said; certain points of view will not be maintained or defended—at least as they could have been. We need to ask: "How is a particular actor distinct from the others? What will he or she do or say that the others will not?" These are very different questions from: "Which one is more important than the others?"

We are not talking about a blurring of the boundaries among the various designations of minister within the church. Rather, we are calling for clarity and crispness. While from one perspective some say that the bishop, priest, and deacon forever remain in the lay order (and the bishop remains a priest and deacon and the priest, a deacon), I think this assertion is confusing to a clear understanding of ministry. I am convinced that it is more useful to separate the four orders according to their differences. The paradox is that as we work to define specifically the ministry of one, the ministries of the other three become more apparent in their own right. As those in each order—lay person, bishop, priest, and deacon—take up their roles within the community with clarity, authority, confidence, and enthusiasm, the others are better able to understand and assume their own.

In the catechism the description of each of these roles begins by saying that persons are to "represent Christ and his Church...." This is what we have in common, and these words have ramifications for us all—lay and ordained—as baptized Christians. A minister is one who follows Jesus, who learns from the example of Jesus and who takes seriously the implications of the baptismal vows to say and to do on Jesus' behalf, to speak and behave as Jesus would.

At baptism we are given both the means and the mandate: we are incorporated into Christ's body, infused with the character of Christ, and given power to represent Christ and his body, the church. We hear the words:

> John...Frances...Sarah...David, you are sealed by the Holy Spirit in Baptism and marked as Christ's own for ever.

Sealed and marked—washed in waters of new life, seared with fire of the spirit, drowned and burned so that we can emerge fresh and new to be about the work God has intended since the beginning of time.

Then the people of the community give the welcome and the charge:

> We receive you into the household of God. Confess the faith of Christ crucified, proclaim his resurrection, and share with us in his eternal priesthood. You are one of us now. You are to go forth with the liberating word of the One who came among us to show us how it is to be. You are now among his own, those ordained as his servants to the world.

So we become members of the company of Christ. We can be with them forever. We can share their tea and cake. We can be shaped by their holy habits. We can hear their lively stories that help us form our own. This company will call us to take up various roles on their behalf—to sit in various chairs on the porch. Then, putting these roles aside until we return, we are to go forth to other companies and other porches, carrying with us as God's baptized people the good news of God in Christ.

Much has been written and said in recent years about ministry, particularly the ministry of all the baptized. The subject is an urgent one, and yet we continue to skirt around it. I suspect one reason we do is that it *is* so urgent. If we took it seriously we would have to change much about how we set priorities and how we live our lives—as a people and as individuals. *There is that cross in the way.*

I think our other primary difficulty is that of definition. The children in our midst have asked: "What are we to *do* if we are followers of Jesus? What habits do we practice?" But what if this is a subsequent question and not the initial one? The children in our midst are only following our lead.

Many of us in the church—volunteer and stipendiary—would say we see our work as ministry. And sadly, we still tend to consider the church as the locus of *real* ministry—despite our many words to the contrary. Nevertheless, we could go on to describe other ministries: of the teacher, of the doctor and the nurse, of the parent. But suppose ministry did not have as much to do with role and function as with who we are and how we are disposed to behave—our "am-ness" as a young woman said to me recently. Suppose the children's question were to become, "Who are we to *be* if we are followers of Jesus? Who are we to become?"

John the baptizer urges us to prepare for this becoming. The derivation of the word "prepare" is illuminating. Not only does it point us to the expected Latin *parare*, to bring order, to get ready, it also refers us to *parere*, to bear, to bring forth. Preparation does not just have to do with getting ready for a birth; it has to do with the very act of birthing itself, with the bringing forth of something which has not been before—something new. As God planted the divine seed into the womb of Mary the virgin, God has planted the divine seed within each of us. Our life's work is to carry that seed, to swell with that seed, to give birth to the fruit of our loving relationship with God: to become the selves we are and were intended to be.

If we took seriously that every one of us is born in the image of the divine and that we bear the mark of the Creator God from before the moment of our birth, the mark peculiarly seared upon us who are named Christian at the time of our baptism...

If we took seriously that every Christian carries deep within herself or himself the mind and heart of Christ and that our lifelong work is to practice holy habits that reveal and name the Christ in ourselves and others—to uncover the image, to scrape away the layers of accumulated grime and turn ourselves to God's polishing hand...

We then would seek perceptions of ministry which include every man, woman, and baby we graft into the body with that marking and sealing and drowning and searing, regardless of gift or grace or circumstance.

We would identify and honor the ministry of the child and of the aged.

We would identify and honor the ministry of the student as well as that of the teacher, the ministry of the listener as well as of the speaker, the ministry of those with lesser intellectual ability as well as of those who labor to give them tools for comprehension and expression.

We would name and respect the ministry of the sick and of the dying as well as of those who bring healing and comfort, the ministry of the homeless as well as of those who strive to bring them some measure of dignity and relief.

We would accept and welcome the ministry of the loyal dissidents in our midst as well as of those who strive to address their concerns, the ministry of those who ask disturbing and annoying questions, the ministry of those who want to change the rules.

Ministry would be part and parcel of our saying, "I am; I am baptized." In describing ministry, questions relating to character, identity, and disposition to behave would concern us before those regarding the various roles we assume or functions we perform. Such an approach could enable us to pass through the strangling sphincters of the "isms"—clericalism, sexism, racism, classism, ageism, and the rest. It is worth a try—*but there is that cross in the way.*

Sunlight

— Do you turn to Jesus Christ and accept
him as your Savior? —

THERE WAS A TIME *in my early twenties when the world I
knew as predictable and orderly fell apart. The sun went
dark for a while, and I was bombarded by doubt. All
that I had been brought up to believe about good and
about God came into question. But because I had been
brought up to believe certain things about God---basic
things like, God is---I took my terrifying questions to a
wise priest of the church, and he introduced me to the
writings of C. S. Lewis. It was a graceful match.*

*One night as I sat up in bed reading, I came to the fol-
lowing passage in the chapter of* Mere Christianity *entitled "The Shocking Alternative":*

I am trying here to prevent anyone saying the really
foolish thing that people often say about Him: "I'm
ready to accept Jesus as a great moral teacher, but I
don't accept His claim to be God." That is the one thing
we must not say. A man who was merely a man and said
the sort of things Jesus said would not be a great moral
teacher. He would either be a lunatic—on a level with
the man who says he is a poached egg—or else he would
be the Devil of Hell. You must make your choice. Either
this man was, and is, the Son of God: or else a madman
or something worse. You can shut Him up for a fool,
you can spit at Him and kill Him as a demon; or you can
fall at His feet and call Him Lord and God. But let us

not come with any patronizing nonsense about His being a great human teacher. He has not left that open to us. He did not intend to.

The hair on my arms rose, and my eyes filled with tears. The choice was suddenly obvious to me. I closed the book and slept soundly for the first time in months. My questions and doubts were not swept away forever that night, and over the years new ones have arisen. But ever since, such questions and doubts have been stripped of any demonic and paralytic power they might hold over me. That night was what some might call a conversion—not to be the last for me. I describe it as a watershed: the night my life stream turned to flow in its true direction. It was a night that the sun shone.

Peter's declaration in Caesarea Philippi regarding Jesus' identity is also a watershed event; its accounting is the pivotal passage of Mark's gospel. Jesus' Galilean ministry is essentially over. He and the twelve are on the road to Jerusalem and all that lies ahead. In the bright light of the moment Jesus invites the disciples to reflect on their experiences with him. He invites them to draw meaning from all that has happened to and around them. "Who do people say that I am?" he asks. "What's out there? What's the latest word?" And they provide him with a variety of interesting responses: He is John the Baptist, some say, and others, Elijah, and still others, one of the prophets. Answers abound as we troop along in the sun.

But "What's out there?" is not the relevant question, and Jesus' next query penetrates to the core of the matter: "But who do you say that I am?" Peter answers correctly for the twelve: "You are the Messiah." Jesus' response at first seems strange. He sternly orders them not to tell anyone. "Why not?" they must have wondered. "It's time to shout from rooftops. You are the one for whom we have been waiting. You are to set everything right again. You are to make up for everything that has gone wrong for our people for so many years!" Still Jesus invokes deep silence, for the disciples do not yet understand the implications of Peter's confession. And we too will be wise to sit in quiet expectation until we have some grasp of what it means for us.

Then Jesus begins to teach. He describes what lies in store for him——suffering, rejection, and death, and the incomprehensible notion of resurrection. Like a developing eclipse, a shadow begins to move across Peter's sunlit declaration. A silhouette falls over the confession made by the young woman lying on her bed those years ago and the one we make each time we reaffirm our faith with the familiar words of the creed:

We believe in one Lord, Jesus Christ,
the only Son of God,
eternally begotten of the Father,
God from God, Light from Light....

For our confessions of belief are not where we end; instead, they mark a beginning. Once we have some glimmer of who Jesus is, we then will be confronted by the implications of the life of discipleship. "No," Peter cries, "No!" And we join him. Jesus is talking dangerous nonsense. No one willingly walks into that kind of future. Maybe he is a crazy man, and we would be crazier to follow him. Peter desperately tries to stop Jesus from saying more. Peter tries to push back the cruciform shadow that continues to move over the sun, but to no avail. It slides ever farther across.

In a sharp rebuke that recalls the wilderness temptation, Jesus retorts to Peter: "Get behind me, Satan! Move back, you seductive devil! You are to follow me, not to lead. The ways of the world are not the ways of God.

God's definition of success may not be yours. God's defi-nition of power may not be yours. God's definition of life may not be yours." We strain to see in the lengthening shade. "What's happening to the sun?" we cry.

Jesus continues unrelentingly. He beckons the crowd to move around him, and he pronounces God's truth. It comes in the form of paradox, as truth usually does:

If any want to become my followers, let them deny themselves and take up their cross and follow me. For those who want to save their life will lose it, and those who lose their life for my sake, and the sake of the gos-pel, will save it.

We are not to talk about the cross; we are to take it up. But taking up the cross does not mean bravely, stoically, cheerfully bearing the burdens and tragedies life throws our way. Any human being can do that. Rather, the disci-ple of Jesus is to deliberately choose what could be avoided----without considering the cost, without worrying about who gets the credit----in order to serve.

Taking up the cross of Christ is putting ourselves with-out reservation in the service of God and neighbor. It is engaging with the world's suffering because we can do nothing less. It is being vulnerable even to those who will turn against us. To deny self----the grasping, self-centered ego----is to liberate the true self----the wondrous one cre-ated in the image of God and baptized into the likeness of Christ. The shadow passes from the sun's face, and we stand in blazing light.

All the Baptized

— I baptize you in the name of the Father,
and of the Son, and of the Holy Spirit. —

WHEN I AM HONEST *with myself, I admit to a recurring
desire to be successful even when I am not sure what
"successful" means. I want to do something someone will
notice, something that will make a difference, something
that will merit a headline somewhere. So I am both relieved and troubled when I read of Jesus' response to the
request of James and John, made as they travel the road
to Jerusalem----on the way to the cross. Jesus is striding
out ahead of the twelve. James and John catch up with
him to ask a favor: "Grant us to sit, one at your right
hand and one at your left, in your glory."*

*And Jesus replies, "To sit at my right or left is not mine
to grant. But you do not know what you are asking. Are
you able to drink the cup that I drink or be baptized with
the baptism with which I am baptized? You must be buried with me in order to live. You must drown in the deep
waters of my love to be free from all that binds and de-
stroys you."*

*"We are able," James and John assure him, all too
quickly----just as we can make and affirm our baptismal
vows without thinking about their terrible implications.
"So be it; it is the only way," Jesus answers. The other ten
are indignant at the presumption of James and John, and
Jesus continues, "The great among you must be servant
and slave of all."*

But in our day----as in the day of the twelve----we do the opposite. What counts is being up front, applauded, recognized, cheered; leading the league; head of the class; top of the line; beating out all competitors by a mile----so what the price of stress?

We have been brought up in a culture in which success is achievement and failure is unacceptable, a culture that has taught us well the importance of being effective, of making it, of being number one. And each of us has made it in our own way. Buried in a box in the attic of our hearts is the trophy for which we worked so hard, gave up so much. Hanging on the wall of our souls is the yellowing certificate for which we sacrificed more than we really had.

We hurry on past Jesus' words about suffering and serving, not because they are obvious or naive but because they indict and offend us. They startle us and whirl us around and nail us to the wall. We are afraid they just might be true. So we go back to fighting among ourselves for position, spinning futilely on our merry-go-rounds, unwilling to make them stop, unwilling to get off.

But Jesus is not giving crazy instruction that makes no sense or damning instruction that, like the brass ring, eludes our grasp. Jesus promises us his presence: "I have come to serve. I am with you. Do as I do. This is the way you were created to live----face to face with each other and face to face with me. It is the only way. I will show you how. I will serve you with my death for you. It is enough."

It is a startling word from Jesus about how we are to live as a baptized, reborn people called to be a sign of God's presence and activity, to be a witness to God's reign; called to be engaged in the ministry of Christ to those denied the benefits and blessings of God's rule. It is a word sometimes difficult to comprehend, let alone live faithfully, for our typical experience of the most radical act the church can perform----baptism----can deceive us.

Many of us remember a time when infants were baptized at private family events and godparents were chosen not because of faithful living, but because they were relatives or friends. The date was rarely remembered or celebrated, as birthdays and other events assumed greater importance. What all too often followed was a time of spotty attendance at church school, during which children in effect were excommunicated and parents led to believe they were fulfilling their baptismal promises. Adolescents were prepared with a crash course in Bible, theology, and Episcopal practice for confirmation, a family puberty rite which made them Episcopalians and gave them the right to commune but which was in fact a graduation exercise. Although conventions are changing today, vestiges of the past remain, and too often there is little in the church's ongoing practice that holds up the significance of baptism for us now.

All this is so different from the experience of the early church, in which it took adults three or more years of preparation and testing to determine whether or not they were living a faithful Christian life. Then at an elaborate liturgy at the Great Vigil of Easter they were drowned in a tomb-like baptismal font, dressed in white clothing, anointed with oil, confirmed, and invited to participate in their first Eucharist. From then on, their baptismal day was remembered and celebrated.

Through the year we come to celebrate together and to reaffirm the significance of baptism. We gather to be reminded that through baptism we died to the world and its ways and were reborn to new life and a new way of living. Even so, we allow our culture to pervade the church, and our competitiveness distorts our understanding of ministry. We the church often eliminate or *discourage whatever does not grow, become cost effective, bring obvious change to people and systems, give results----results that can bring us honor and glory. But Jesus never said, "Be effective." He said, "Live with me; live for each other." And God favors the outsider, the outcast, so Jesus invites us to join him in their midst.*

I recently met a woman whose actions do not make sense if we are talking about visible change and results. Her name is Meg, and she told me about her introduction to the nursing home where her mother, a victim of Alzheimer's, finally had to go. There she found a largely deserted population, forsaken by family, doctors, and clergy.

Meg goes to the nursing home every Sunday morning to lead worship there for fourteen Episcopalians. She takes a cross from the parish school where she works and places it on a table she has covered with a white cloth. That's all. And then she plays grand works like Handel's Messiah *and the last movement of Beethoven's choral symphony. Believe it or not, the little group gathered in their wheelchairs around the table begin to stir. Stilled voices begin to murmur little fragments of song. Dulled eyes flicker with tiny sparks of recognition. Sagging faces lift in a measure of expression. And the words of the worship service they anticipate and love to repeat with Meg are, "for the means of grace and for the hope of glory"!*

I have a crucifix hanging on the wall of my study. Nailed to the walnut cross is an abstract human form. Toward the top of the figure is a stone, a white and red ringed agate. A tear of blood drips from this eye of God, the eye which sees all the hurt and broken ones of the world----confused, unfaithful followers; victims of greed and the misuse of power; those caught in illness and in violence not of their doing; Meg and you and me.

And because we are held fast in the sight of this suffering eye from the height of that cross----even when it must seem to God to make no difference----we receive power to live lives that seem to make no sense by the standards of the world. God loves us indiscriminately and with abandon. God becomes an outcast from all that we consider effective, useful, and successful. "This is what it is like to be mine," God tells us; God is for us. "You too will suffer. But in that suffering, you will find life. You will meet yourself as you truly are----one created in my image."

The choice is ours. At our baptism we learned the truth about ourselves and how God wills us to live. We spend the rest of our lives living into this truth and making eucharist for God's care of us----for grace that bathes us with the clean water of divine blood; grace that removes the heavy hearts of stone from our breasts and replaces them with hearts of warm and pulsing flesh; grace that revives our lifeless fantasies and grafts us into God's breathing, dreaming body of vitality and hope; grace that frees us from our drives to be effective and adequate. Over and again at this table we are to be reconstituted as Christ's body, taken up into God's reign, and sent back with a renewed vision of God's intention for us and the gifts and graces necessary to live accordingly.

The merry-go-round slows down, and we can get off.

Dispositions

---- Fill them with your holy and life-giving Spirit. ----

RECENTLY I WAS TOLD that a friend of mine had spread hurtful rumors about another friend. The first words out of my mouth were, "I don't believe it!" Such behavior just did not sound like her. It is not part of her character as I have experienced it over the many years we have known each other. Quite the contrary, my friend goes out of her way to look for something positive to say about everyone—even when I think she is being overly "creative"! Another way of describing this aspect of my friend is to say that she is not disposed to gossip; rather, her disposition is to look for grace.

The word "disposition" is derived from the Latin *disponere*, to arrange or to put in order. As Christians, we are fully human as we are disposed to imitate Christ. Another word for these Christ-like dispositions is "virtues." I was describing my grandmother's character— her dispositions—when I thought about why it was her porch the good Methodist ladies chose day after day.

Considering ministry from the perspective of character and disposition *before* role and function can offer us a fresh entrance into the urgent but elusive question regarding its nature. Our ministry then becomes the particular way we order life and put together our lives according to our foundational orientation. For Christians, this orientation is found as we look to be like Jesus, and thus to reflect the image of God.

We cannot stop there, however. The ordering or arrangement of our being is made manifest or visible to others by our behavior, by what we do and by how we explain why we do it. So it follows that the outward and visible form our ministry takes will be shaped by where and when we were born, the composition of our genes, where we grew up and went to school, and so forth. *How* we give flesh and blood to the mind and heart of Christ is influenced by time and place and opportunity. Nevertheless, our lifelong work as baptized persons—to live into ever-deepening relationship with God and neighbor—is not fundamentally dependent upon circumstance or role.

Rather, our ministry is an expression of our character, our identity, and our disposition to behave in Christ-like ways. So perceived, ministry is possible for all baptized persons regardless of the circumstances in which they find themselves, regardless of the gifts and graces which are theirs. We then have an understanding of ministry which can break the bondages of role and function, and can be claimed outside the confines of the institutional church. It is this perception of ministry that is so needed by a world in distress.

What follows is a list of dispositions that are poured over and into us at baptism, marked on our foreheads by the Spirit's hand. They are called forth in the particular contexts of our lives, as we strive to proclaim by word and example the good news of God in Christ. They are virtues or dispositions necessary if we are to follow Jesus, if we are to become what and who our baptism says we are: Christ's body, Christ's presence in the world.

Disposed to be present
We stand still in the moment, in order to see what is hidden from our busy, darting eyes. We attend to the ac-

tivity of the divine in our midst, or hear the awful silence of God's absence in the face of our sin. We are aware of those around us, others who also are created in the image of God; we look each other in the eye, honoring one another with attention. Further, we are alert to the creation as a whole: all we see, hear, taste, touch, and smell; each blade of grass, fashioned by the divine hand and worthy of care and respect. We approach the world and its creatures as subjects to be cherished, not objects to be examined and studied at arm's length.

To those who are disposed to be present, the simplest of gestures takes on profound possibility, and every moment is pregnant with opportunity to bring healing and liberation or to bring destruction and death. It is said that the young Desmond Tutu was in part set on the course of his life's work when he saw a white Anglican priest tip his hat in respect to Tutu's black South African mother. We are to tip our hats to those we encounter along the way. We are to greet one another with holy blessing.

A colleague of mine once described a ministry of presence. A congregation was in severe conflict; they had reached the end of any and all ropes. It was the rector's last Sunday, and my friend decided to be there. On that day he would not lead discussions or teach; such would come later. He would simply be present. And he was—for three services and two coffee hours. Several people later told him that his continuing presence throughout the morning became a symbol of support and care for everyone involved: "You were showing us that we are not alone." My friend's task that day was to stand with those people in their suffering, to evidence compassion: *compati*, to suffer together.

Of the handful of words that characterize the life and person of Jesus, two are presence and compassion. The

Samaritan woman at the well. The hemorrhaging woman who touched the fringe of his clothes. The man born blind. The children. The hungry multitudes. Even the Pharisees.

> *The children in our midst look around and ask (as those children always will): "Where are we to stand? What are we to see? What will we miss if we do not?"*

Disposed to be vulnerable

The Latin root of "vulnerable" is *vulnerare*, to wound. Vulnerability is not our seeking to be wounded because woundedness in itself is good and desirable. Instead, it has to do with willingness to be wounded for the sake of the other, in service to the other, and to allow those wounds to show rather than to hide behind a mask of rigid adequacy and slick confidence. It is a willingness to become frayed around the edges of our hearts, without plucking frantically at loosened threads, tucking them in and out of sight.

Vulnerability has to do with trusting God and others, with taking off our shoes so weary and filthy feet can be washed by a neighbor on Jesus' behalf. It has to do with heeding Jesus' words to Peter: "Unless I wash you, you have no share with me."

Vulnerability has to do with generosity, being generous with all that we have and are and which does not belong to us in the first place. The word "generous" is derived from *genus*, birth. Would anyone deny the vulnerability of the birthing posture?

Vulnerability has to do with emptying ourselves so we can receive, of forgiving ourselves and others so we can move on, so our feet are not mired in despair. It has to do with being dispensable so we can be dispensed on behalf of the reign of God, so we can go forth into the world to love and to serve. It has something and every-thing to do with a cross.

Babies and children know vulnerability until we teach them that it is not attractive or mature to be so. The poor, the sick, and the aged can know of vulnerability until we make them ashamed of it.

> *The children in our midst look around and ask (as those children always will): "Whom are we to trust? What are we to risk? Whom are we to for-give?"*

Disposed to be hospitable

We are inclined to welcome, to take others in. Hospi-tality comes from *hostis*, as does the word "hostile." In this light, hospitality entails welcoming the enemy as guest. The enemy is all that is strange and different and frightening to us: ideas, people, change, endings, begin-nings—even the pursuing and beckoning God with whom we continually wrestle and contend.

A hospice nurse talked of ministry among the dying, including herself in their number. "We are learning to-gether to welcome the enemy death as guest," she said.

One of our college chaplains told me about a young man attending her university. His name is Jonathan, and she is concerned about her responsibility to him and to the church. Jonathan prides himself on being a card-car-rying agnostic, and he does so with great integrity. He is quite willing to attend services on special occasions with his parents; he just does not say or sing a word during them. On the other hand, he takes just about every re-ligion course offered and keeps showing up on the chap-lain's doorstep, wanting to debate religious questions with an intensity that indicates more than intellectual curiosity. "It's as if he were in a wrestling match with

God," the chaplain said. "I have decided that my job is to applaud the match but stay out of their way."

Jonathan might scoff at my words, but I think he is engaging in the work of hospitality. He is risking encountering the One who will change his life. Like Jacob, he will walk away limping, but he will have a new name.

As baptized disciples we are to wrestle with the enemy and the stranger. We are to help others as they wrestle for themselves, knowing when to applaud and stay out of the way. With Jesus we are to invite the tax collectors and sinners to our table. We are to listen to the disturbing words of Canaanite women as they call us to define our work in new and faithful ways, as they point us into God's way: "Yes, Lord, yet even the dogs eat the crumbs that fall from the master's table. Your responsibility goes beyond the house of Israel. Your mission extends further than the familiarity of today." We are to pray the agonizing words of the garden: "Not my will but yours be done." At baptism we receive the new name—Christian—and we are to spend the rest of our lives welcoming its implications as our guest.

> *The children in our midst look around and ask (as those children always will): "Who is asking questions and making demands we do not want to hear? What does it mean to limp? Will we have new names? What might they be?"*

Disposed to bring order

Ah, this one we can claim, we who are the designated orderers of the church. (Some of us are even called ordained!) But we are wise to exercise care just at those times when definitions seem clearest: we may be interjecting our own inadequate notions of order in the place of more faithful understanding.

I remember a bag lady named Rosemary who raised questions about order for a number of good church people. Rosemary made her home for years in the sprawling physical plant of a cathedral church. An elegant woman with a sad story to tell, she moved from room to room during the imposed inconvenience of the business day. Rosemary attended services regularly in her home, slipping into the congregation without a ripple. She slept on couches at night and showered in an upstairs bathroom. Although she did borrow a clock so she could regulate her activities and took modest helpings of food from the kitchen pantry, she disturbed nothing of real value in all the time she lived there. An early arrival finally discovered Rosemary asleep in an office. She was asked to leave, and the cathedral's order was restored. Its good people made offers of assistance to her, but she refused them all. I believe she chose to look for a new home more fitting to her own sense of order.

We are to take care that we do not equate order with maintenance of the status quo, or with lining up our lives in tight and rigid rows. Rather, we need to see order as fluidity and motion—the ordering of Van Gogh and Mozart, or the child with finger paints and paper. The ordering of the poet and the storyteller.

A story is told about Michelangelo. He was found chipping away at a block of marble. When he was asked what he was carving, Michelangelo answered, "I am not carving anything; I am releasing the angel from the stone." Bringing order is not imposing form from without; it is aiding the form concealed within to emerge—from stones and from the souls of children.

Most profoundly, ordering involves pursuing the will of God and participating in God's reign of reconciliation and abundance. It involves courage—the fortitude to keep at the task and not to give in or give up, not to lose hope. To order is to question: to assume that answers are imaginable. To order is to speak in prophetic tones, in utterances calling us both forward and back to God's design. It is to reveal alternatives, to confront. It is to cry, "Things do not have to be the way they appear; they were *never* supposed to be this way."

Jesus brought order by turning the expected upside down, inside out. His order is the order of paradox: to be greatest is to be least, the servant of all. Rules are to be broken so that God's law of love can be declared. The blind see, and the sighted are blind. Power is dying on a cross.

> *The children in our midst look around and ask (as those children always will): "What is hiding inside the stone? How are things supposed to be?"*

Disposed to be outrageously humble

We maintain perspective and a sense of humor; we allow ourselves to laugh and to play. Jesus said, "Come to me as children come, fresh and without layers of pretense." So many of his parables are based in humor and plays on words, but we miss the point; we do not laugh. Jesus tells us not to take ourselves so seriously. While we are God's servants to the world, the coming of the reign of God does not lie in our hands. God's reign is here, and lightness of touch can be its most faithful witness: God uses the ridiculous to convert deadly serious hearts.

A few days before our diocesan convention several years ago, the scene was all too familiar: fuses were short, copy machines were on overload, and any humor took the form of barbs. The tension could be cut with that proverbial knife, until relief appeared in the form of Nellie Hearn, laundress for the cathedral and its resident theologian. She sized up the situation in a flash.

Throwing her head back and her arms heavenward, she cried out in mock disbelief with a voice that penetrated walls: "For *this* you died?"

Humility involves knowing oneself—gifts, graces, and limitations—and then walking on the ground, the *humus*, of that knowledge. It is practicality and prudence, holding us in place and preventing our sailing away into flights of fantasy. It means turning loose the fierce need to control everyone and everything as if we were in charge of history's course.

My grandmother, my Nanno, was dying. I received the call while at work and raced to reach her before she slipped away from us at age ninety-six. Her last words on this earth were directed to me as I entered the room and took her hand. "Well, you're here, Lady; I'm glad you were able to make it." She was the hostess, and I, the guest of honor. Her mouth curved in the familiar mischievous grin, her weary eyes twinkled, and she died. The joke was on me. I threw back my head and laughed and laughed—before I cried.

> *Still again the children in our midst look around and ask (as those children will continue to do): "Does God laugh with us? Does God shed tears when we cry?"*

Disposed to simplify

When Jesus sent out the disciples two by two, he charged them to wear sandals and one tunic and to carry a staff. They were to take nothing else for the journey: neither bread nor bag nor money in their belts. The work of the followers of Jesus requires simplicity, of being unencumbered and stripped so they can move lightly on their feet into the world's sometimes perplexing maze, unburdened so they can dance sprightly steps of healing and freedom and hope. Judicious pruning is to be our watchword, temperance our path. We are to trim our unruly branches. We are to cut back our excesses so these Christ-like dispositions can emerge and flower and we can go forth to love and serve.

Yet we as a church are loathe to eliminate so growth can occur. Instead we continue to collude with the culture: we speak of success rather than of faithfulness, and we define this success as bigger than before and more than ever. We fill time with churchy busyness and activity and do not set one another free to bear witness to Christ wherever we may be. Clutter added to clutter. I have heard the church compared to a vacuum cleaner that sucks its people in and whirls them around, flattening them against spinning walls.

I wonder how we as a body could reveal the simplicity we are to assume in our personal lives? I wonder what would it mean for us to go on the journey—as a church and as individuals—with a staff, a pair of sandals, and one tunic?

> *The children in our midst ask: "What is too much? What must we take with us? What can we cut?"*

The list of dispositions—virtues—can go on. I am sure we can add others from our experience and imagination and from our rich heritages of Scripture and tradition. But we are to remember that the divine image—for Christians, the mind and heart of Christ—is the combination of all the dispositions. They must be held in tension with each other for the whole to be complete. The binding force is love.

Danger

— Open their hearts to your grace and truth. —

IT IS RISKY TO GET INVOLVED with other travelers as we move along the road. The disciples encounter the Canaanite woman and see her as pushy, aggressive, impertinent, brash. They beg Jesus to send her away. Not only is her persistence irritating, she isn't even one of them. A despised outsider like her does not merit the attention she is receiving. A group of onlookers has gathered.

Besides, haven't they withdrawn into the Gentile region for a much-needed rest? Jesus has had yet another confrontation with a swarm of Pharisees and scribes, trying to sting him with their wearisome questioning. His breaks with their rules are becoming dangerous. And then he showed his impatience with Peter's simple request for an explanation. Yes, a rest is in order. The woman must be dismissed.

But she is not so much pushy and impertinent as she is desperate. Watching the demon seize her child with racking violence has become unbearable. She aches in her helplessness and frustration. "If only I could take it upon myself; if only there were something I could do!"

Maybe there is. She has heard of the young Jewish teacher, the one who dares to speak with compelling authority to the Jewish elders. Stories of healings have passed even into Tyre and Sidon. They say he can heal with his very word. And he is here. "If only I could talk to him, look him in the eye; if only...."

She sees him sitting on the ground, off by himself, back against a scruffy tree. She wraps her cloak around herself, takes a deep breath, and approaches. Boldly invoking the Messianic title, she moves right to her purpose:

> *"Have mercy on me, Lord, Son of David; my daughter is tormented by a demon."*

> *"I stand before you, Lord, Son of David. I know who you are. Help."*

> *"I meet your eyes with mine, Lord, Son of David. Look."*

> *"I seek your word, Lord, Son of David. Speak."*

And there is silence. Jesus is startled by this Gentile woman's insight. How can she see when no one else seems able? He ventures a few quick glances in her direction, then looks down at his hands. His fingers tense involuntarily. He says nothing.

The disciples come to his rescue. "Send her away or she will continue to follow us with that annoying cry. We don't need this right now." Jesus agrees. He responds with the party line, the predictable answer: "I was sent only to the lost sheep of the house of Israel." That's that. But there is a hint of hesitation in his words.

She drops to her knees in front of him. He feels the bark of the tree as his back stiffens against it. She says calmly, her voice low now in its resolve, "Lord, help me." Silence still, and then he answers. A note of respectful amusement has crept into his voice. "It is not fair to take the children's food and throw it to the dogs."

The woman is equal to his challenge. She rises, plants herself squarely in front of him, and picks up the repartee. "Yes, Lord, yet even the dogs eat the crumbs that fall from their masters' table." She tosses her head back and waits. Her heart has begun to stir.

Jesus rises to his feet as well. There is silence again before he begins to speak----more to himself than to her. "Woman, great is your faith! Let it be done for you as you wish." In that moment her daughter is healed.

We the church will do well to attend to this unsettling story, because an encounter between Jesus and the Canaanite woman becomes our encounter with an unsettling world.

The disciples call the woman pushy, impertinent, brash, and annoying. She calls herself desperate. Jesus calls her faithful. Each is an accurate portrayal, and in her we can see the impertinence and brashness of all those others who come to our door and ask for a word of hope.

They have heard something about us as people of God. They have heard that we bring a message of good news---- even when we do not quite believe it ourselves. They come even though they are not one of us: they are from the wrong background or the wrong class; they are the wrong color or the wrong sexual orientation; they harbor wrong opinions or practice wrong behavior. But they still come with sick children and dashed dreams because there is nowhere else to go. We are their last resort as industries and programs fail, as confidence in leadership erodes, as peace and justice continue to elude them. They come with a persistence born of desperation. They come.

> *"Have mercy on us, Church, Body of Christ; our sons and daughters have no safe place to sleep, and their bellies grind in hunger."*

> *"We stand before you, Church, Body of Christ. We know who you are. We know who you can be. Help."*

"We meet your eyes with ours, Church, Body of Christ. Look."

"We seek your healing word, Church, Body of Christ. Speak."

And too often there is silence; or worse, we give the party line: "We are doing all we can to care for our own. The budget is tight; the economy is bad. We've never done it that way; this is the way it's always been." That's that.

But there is a hint of hesitation in our words. Unless we are dead to our true selves, we know their call upon us is legitimate. Our heritage tells us that we are to open our doors to the outsider, to feed the hungry, to heal the sick, to bring sight to the blind, to free the imprisoned, to give beds to the weary----even when it seems safer and more comfortable to look the other way. So it is by the grace of God that the persistent Canaanite woman shows up at our door, looks us in the eye, and cries her haunting cry: "Help me."

It is a dangerous thing to meet the Canaanite woman. It is a dangerous thing to look her squarely in the eye. It is a dangerous thing to give heed to her voice, to give credence to her demands. We run the risk of being uncomfortable, of being inconvenienced----of sometimes looking silly. We run the risk of changing our direction. We run the risk of being converted. We run the risk of being God's holy people.

Choices

— Do you renounce all sinful desires
that draw you from the love of God? —

*YEARS AGO, WHEN I WAS THE MOTHER of two small boys,
an older friend made a remark I still remember today. "I
do not have much trouble choosing between things that
are clearly 'good' or 'bad,'" she said. "My problem comes
from choosing among things that all seem good."*

*Choices. We all have choices to make, priorities to set.
First, there is what we call our work, and it must be close
to the top of the list. How else could we make the mort-
gage payment, put food on the table and gas in the car? I
work for the church; I am obviously serving others in the
name of Jesus----or so I tell myself. That's why I can give
away so many weekend hours with a clear conscience!*

*And there is personal time----the cooking and cleaning
and driving and shopping time. There are calls to make
and letters to write now that children live in distant
states, now that parents are alone and might fall in the
night. So much to do; so much to do. "Weren't we going to
save one night just to be home together this week?" Better
make another list so that I don't leave off something that
is really important!*

*Then there is community time. Why did I ever agree to
serve on the hospital board? They said they needed someone with my background in planning. And the homeown-
ers' association meeting is coming up. They want one of*

us to run for office. I guess it's our turn, but can we squeeze anything else into the calendar?

And church time. The class I said I'd teach. The salad I promised to prepare for the parish dinner, thinking it would take less time than an entree. Services. Programs. Where is the year going? I keep thinking it will slow down soon----if I make it.

And more and more and more. All good choices. Not a bad one in the bunch. And to complicate the situation, the more we try to do, the more we are praised and rewarded. Yet we know something's out of whack.

Lately the words of my wise friend have reappeared on the pages of my life book----the story of my days that I write in my heart----highlighted and underscored now that energy is not so boundless, now that I am well into middle age, now that I know all too well the fleeting quality of time. Choice-making has become leaner. And as important as choosing well and wisely is to our physical and psychological health, deeper issues are at stake----for us as persons and for us as church.

If we are honest with ourselves, we will confess that we are at the center of many of our "good" choices. We want others to be pleased with us. We want to be pleased with ourselves. We want to appear relevant. We want to be useful. We want to be noticed. We want to make a difference. On and on. Our fragile egos are so vulnerable to the enticements of the evil one.

Listen again to the narrative of the wilderness temptations. Jesus, filled with the Holy Spirit following his own baptism in the Jordan, is led----driven----by that strange spirit into a forty-day ordeal at the hands of the devil. It is a story about making choices, and it offers the plumb line of motive to guide us through our self-imposed snarls of unending motion. It tells us that what we choose is not so much the issue as why.

Three times the devil asks Jesus to choose: to turn stones to bread so he can feed himself and others; to have authority over all nations so he can straighten out the snarl of worldly politics; and to throw himself from the pinnacle of the temple so he can make a spectacular showing and draw immediate attention to his cause. On the surface, not bad choices. But Jesus turns each one of them down because they do not meet the flinty test of God's will. "I do not do my will," Jesus says again and again, "but the will of my Father who sent me." Our choices are to be in line with God's intentions.

Jesus does not refuse to feed hungry mouths during the course of his ministry. Jesus feeds, but he does not do so in order to receive praise and thanks. He feeds because it is God's will that the basic physical needs of God's children be met.

Jesus does not refuse to assert power and authority; rather, he refuses to be powerful according to the world's greed for control and domination. The power of Jesus is love that will suffer on behalf of others.

What Jesus refuses in not throwing himself from the roof of the temple is a sensational act of daring. Instead, he mounts the cross and rises beyond the sway of death forever. If we but follow him, we are set free to do God's work in God's time—forever.

God gives us time. God gives us power. They are gifts to do with when and how God wills. We will not give up responsibility to choose and act if we acknowledge our part in God's reign. Rather, we can then choose and act with peace and confidence, no longer chasing our tails through mazes of frenzied anxiety. But our quest to know the will of God involves our going into the wilderness—cruciform marks on our foreheads—to wrestle with motive and choice, to wrestle for our souls with the evil one who says we can do it on our own. And we dare to wrestle because victory has been assured us.

The road ahead is God's road. It will twist and take strange and marvelous turns. Even when the course of the road moves over territory not in keeping with God's plan, territory that is barren and filled with signs of death and despair, God promises to be with us on the journey. Leon Joseph Cardinal Seuens is quoted: "I believe in surprises of the Holy Spirit....Who would dare to say that the love and imagination of God were exhausted?" To hope, then, is our duty, not a luxury.

We are ever to engage in the activity of patient and hopeful waiting, acknowledging that our only faithful response is to participate in the plan unfolding before and around us. When asked what he would do if told the end of time had come, Martin Luther responded, "I would plant an apple tree." When asked the same question while plowing a field, Saint Francis is said to have replied, "I would make another furrow over there."

Covenant

*---- Will you who witness these vows do all in your power
to support these persons in their life in Christ? ----*

IN AN ADDRESS AT WESTERN Theological Seminary in
1990, Lesslie Newbigin, the former Bishop of South In-
dia and longtime leader in the ecumenical movement,
described a psychiatrist who was also a devout Christian. When she was asked whether her practice of psy-
chiatry helped her in her Christian life, the doctor
responded, "Of course." When she then was asked the
converse question, "Can you bring to bear the insights of
the faith into the consulting room?" she said, "Certainly
not! That would be unprofessional."

The question Newbigin raises for us is crucial to any
consideration of the ministry of the follower of Jesus:
What kind of help is needed if this psychiatrist is to
turn her profession from its allegiance to principalities
and powers and myths and beliefs other than those of
the gospel of Christ? And the same question must be
asked as regards us all—teachers, students, parents, doctors, patients, business leaders, lawyers, laborers, farmers, and on and on.

Like many of us who have been baptized into the
body of Christ, this good doctor is finding difficulty
connecting her life in the church with the other dimen-
sions of her life. To say it another way, the promises she
has made at baptism are not promises that guide her
everyday experience. Again, I think the trap of seeing

ministry primarily as role and function rather than as basic orientation holds her fast—as it does most of us.

Using the compelling metaphor of an undercover agent, Newbigin went on to challenge the local congregation to assume its responsibility of equipping members for public life that is informed by the Christian faith. He suggested such equipping involves fashioning them as subversives who are able to work from within and to bring the powers that be back into allegiance with Christ. He reminded us that the work of undercover agents, of subversives, takes a great deal of skill.

But the answer does not lie in proper instruction, in teaching correct definition. Rather, it has to do with the totality of our life in community, with all the ways we live and worship and learn together. If these dispositions are to become part of our character, we all need to participate in the life of a community that embodies them. Our responsibility to each other in the company of faith is to name the dispositions out of which we behave in Christ-like ways, to create an environment in which they can be seen and formed, to help each other practice holy habits and make faithful choices, and to hold each other accountable when we do not.

In community, children—and adults—will not learn about presence and vulnerability and hospitality and the rest so much as they will experience others' living in a certain way and will want to do so themselves. Then they will know the silence necessary for insight. They will be asked to slow down so someone can catch up. They will see the tears of teachers so they can cry their own. They will be encouraged to ask new questions. Their answers will be heard and respected. They will participate in the community's meal of grateful thanksgiving.

And just as the child on the porch heard stories that told her of her heritage and shaped who she would become, we are to fill the air with precious and sacred words so that our children—and we—can know who God intends us to be. We are to be daring communities of storytellers and storyhearers, people who understand the power of the word among us and who both embrace that word and catch our breath with surprise in its presence.

We are to be communities that practice the art of critical reflection. Telling about the events of our lives and those of others is not enough. We are to look at those stories, to hold them up for testing and scrutiny, to examine them for meaning, to measure them against the constant plumb lines of Scripture, tradition, and reason so we can resist the popular seductions of our culture—the consumer and shopping mall mentalities that entice and coopt us. The dispositions described earlier do not reflect worldly success and power. They do not adhere to the popular interpretation of strong and powerful as mighty and forceful. Rather, they reflect the image of one who demonstrated power as dying on a cross.

We are to offer more faithful definitions of reality— God's reality—and we are to be communities that live and tell the truth, with God's help. We cannot be such communities as long as we make and remake promises we do not help each other to keep. The baptismal covenant is central. If we are not intentional about keeping these promises and then helping others to do so as well, we are an immoral people at our very core.

Again, looking at our ministry as a question of character rather than one of role is useful. While there is no neat way to connect a disposition with one of the promises we make at baptism and make again each time we reaffirm our vows, I think the dispositions are enmeshed in them.

Wouldn't it be difficult to continue in the apostles' teaching and fellowship, in the breaking of bread, and in the prayers if one were not disposed to be vulnerable?

And wouldn't it be difficult to persevere in resisting evil and to repent and return if one were not disposed to be hospitable—to welcome the enemy as guest?

Wouldn't it be difficult to proclaim the good news by word and example if one were not disposed toward simplicity—and humility?

Wouldn't it be difficult, if not impossible, to seek and serve Christ in all persons and to love them—*love them*—if one were not disposed to be present to them and see their beauty?

And wouldn't it be impossible to strive for justice and peace and to respect the dignity of all people if one were not disposed to bring order—to cry with the voice of the prophet, "Things do not have to be the way they appear to be; things are *never* the way they appear to be!"?

To be such companies of habit and story and truth-telling requires that we also be communities of patience. We are to practice the exercise of waiting. We are to know that time is God's, not our own. We are to live into rhythms of gestation, of carrying, enduring, embracing. God will keep God's part of the covenant with us. For this we are ever to be grateful and to give thanks—to make eucharist. The question is whether or not we will keep our covenant with God and with each other.

Broken Promises

— Let us join with those who are committing themselves to
Christ and renew our own baptismal covenant. —

WE HAVE NO BUSINESS asking promises of people that we
will not assist them in keeping. We say we will do all in
our power to support each other in our life in Christ. The
word "obliged" is useful here. Derived from obligare, to
bind to, it speaks of our mutual responsibility based in
baptism's binding. We are obligated to one another because we have participated in a common ordination to
serve as Christ's representatives wherever we find ourselves. We are connected by cords of love.

Before his death, Joshua gathered all the tribes of Israel at Shechem to renew their covenant with God. "Thus
says the Lord," Joshua begins, and he recounts the story
of God's activity in their lives: "Long ago I took your father Abraham and your mother Sarah...." It is our story
as well, only we add to it all that has happened on both
sides of those three days in which death became life, and
history was spun around forever.

Joshua concludes his recitation with a challenge:
"Choose today whom you will serve. It is time. The hour
is now." He puts forth that question which never goes
away: "Whom will you serve? Whom will you serve?"
Thus asks God long ago; thus asks God today. "You can
worship the gods of the Amorites in whose land you are
living; you can worship the gods of possession and competition, of food and drink, of health and youth, of educa-

tion and information; the gods of flag and stock market, of fall fashion and sports hero----or you can worship me. Choose now."

The people assure Joshua: "Far be it from us that we should forsake the Lord our God to serve other gods...." And every time someone among us is baptized we make our promises to serve God as well: "Of course we will continue in the apostles' teaching and fellowship, in the breaking of bread, and in the prayers. Of course we will persevere in resisting evil, and when we fall into sin, repent and return. Of course we will proclaim by word and example. Seek and serve Christ in all persons? Of course we will. Strive for justice and peace among all people of this community and the world? Of course----could we do anything else?"

Dangerous, indicting promises made before God and each other.

Long ago Joshua cautioned the people of Israel about making promises. "I don't think you will keep your word," he contends. "Oh, but we can," they respond. "If you make this covenant and then break it you will be witnesses against yourselves," he warns, "for God will not deal lightly with those who break the covenant." "We know what we are doing," they reassure him, and the covenant is made.

Do we dare dismiss this as a quaint story about an ancient people around a large stone under a faded oak at Shechem, or should we shiver a little because we know how the story turns out? We know the people of Israel did not come close to keeping those words of faithfulness to God in the seductive land of Canaan. We know about their continuing betrayal and about unheeded warnings of prophets and long years of captivity in exile.

But the shiver that sends shudders through our souls---- if we allow ourselves to feel it----has more to do with our own graveyard of broken and maimed promises. Promises made to God, to each other, to self.

Continue in fellowship and prayer? Resist evil? Proclaim by word and example? Seek and serve Christ at all times and everywhere? Strive for justice and peace? Respect the dignity of every human being? Some days we have no idea what to do with these words. Some days we are clear about their implications but the price of living into them cuts across our self-interest----personally, communally, nationally.

Promises. Remember those solemn pacts of childhood, sealed with mutual smearing of drops of blood? "We'll be best friends forever!" Now long years of absence cast their shadows in between.

What about those promises made to ourselves with confidence and hearty determination on the first day of each January----to lose weight, to exercise, to read, to spend more time with the people we love? What about those? Bones in the yard.

And promises made in the dark over the fevered head of a sweating baby. "God, just get him through this, and I will do anything you ask of me." Only we forgot later to ask what that "anything" might be.

Promises two people made before God and community to love and comfort and honor and be faithful, mutually to give until the end of life. But the end of life came in unanticipated ways, and the words spoken did not hold.

Promises made to God and each other when we marked someone as Christ's own forever, a member of that eternal and royal priesthood. "Will you who witness these vows do all in your power to support these persons in their life in Christ?" "We will," we have said automatically, again and again. All in our power? Joshua's words shiver through us anew.

Like the long trek of the people of Israel, our way is paved with good intentions and unkept promises. With Paul we lament: "I do not do what I say I will do, but I do the very things I have sworn not to do again. What hope can there be for me? Who can help me? Or am I lost?" We do not have to be convinced; we indict ourselves with the evidence surrounding us.

But this still is not where the story ends. We are not left to wallow in guilt and quiver in fear. The answer lies in our responses to the baptismal questions. "Will you...?" we are asked. And we reply, "I will, with God's help." With God's help. *Throughout the story of the relationship between God and God's people the word again and again has been: "I love you----I will be with you----I will help you----I promise you----and I do not break my promises." With Paul we can grasp forgiveness and relief: "Thanks be to God through Jesus Christ our Lord!"*

As part of this help God gives us the community of the church, the body of Christ. It is here we can confess our broken promises in the presence of God and each other. It is here we can speak and hear words of pardon and healing. It is here we can ask and answer challenging questions----"Will you? Do you promise?" It is here we can support each other and hold each other accountable. It is here we feed each other with true food and true drink; food of spirit, not of flesh; food that imparts the strength and power to become God's people of promise.

Puzzling? Hard to understand? Yes. John tells us that upon hearing such words from Jesus many disciples turned back and no longer went about with him. Jesus asks the twelve, "Do you wish to go away as well?" Peter's response parallels Joshua's challenge all those centuries before. Joshua asked, "Whom will you choose?" Peter answers with a question and a proclamation: "Where else can we go? You have the words of eternal life."

Gateway

— Do you put your whole trust in his grace and love? —

A FEW YEARS AGO I attended a challenging and difficult conference in St. Louis. I was inspired to survive the week by an ever-present symbol of hope and perseverance: Eero Saarinen's magnificent Gateway Arch. This 630-foot-high, curving span of gleaming stainless steel soars over Gateway Park beside the Mississippi River. It is a monument to all the pioneers who set forth from St. Louis on their way to new life and new opportunity in the West. The arch loomed right outside my hotel window. It was the first thing I saw each morning when I awoke; I watched fireworks play on its polished surface as I lay in bed at night, too wound up and too tired to find sleep. In my imagination I saw thousands of people pouring through it; I even imagined my joining them on a journey of thrilling discovery. Now when I hear the word "gate," I see that arch.

In the tenth chapter of John's gospel, Jesus calls himself the gate for the sheep. At first I thought I had caught him in a mixed metaphor. Just a few verses earlier he has called himself the shepherd, the one who leads the sheep and whose voice alone the sheep know. Now he calls himself the gate. But I was wrong: Jesus is referring to the hillside sheepfolds in Palestine where the sheep stayed the night in the warm season rather than returning to the communal village folds. These hillside folds were merely open spaces enclosed by a rough stone wall. The sheep en-

tered and left through an opening in the wall, one without a door of any sort. At night, after calling his sheep into the fold, the shepherd lay down across this opening, literally becoming the gate. The sheep could not wander out without passing over his body, nor could danger invade the fold.

In naming himself the shepherd of the flock, Jesus could not have picked a better image for the intimacy we are to enjoy with God. Jesus is describing how God is. Jesus is telling us who we are before God. Jesus is promising that our lives are in the hands of a God who knows each of us by name, who considers each of us precious:

> As the shepherd leads his sheep into green pastures, God will lead us where we can fill ourselves full of all that enriches and sustains us, all that challenges and gives us joy, all that is beautiful and true, all that brings us deep peace.

> As the shepherd's voice is the only one the sheep will follow, so God has created in each of us an ear tuned to holy presence, and God promises to keep calling out to us until we are willing to hear.

> As the shepherd goes after and finds even one lost sheep, God is ever in pursuit of us when we wander too far away.

> As the shepherd places his body at the opening of the fold to protect his sheep from the dangers of the night, God's body protects us from the soaring cross, the gateway to our freedom.

That God the good shepherd promises to be with us at gateways is the best of news, for our only certainty is that we do not know what is coming next. Our lives can be described as a series of gateways----of beginnings and endings, of births and deaths, of stops and starts, of moving from familiar places to strange ones. Every breaking morning is a gateway; every falling night is one, too. Gateways are alluring, and they are terrifying. While we are drawn by the power of their mystery, we know that we can encounter disappointment and danger on the other side. Will we find that for which we long, or will there only be dreaded darkness?

Every gateway obviously does not open to green pastures and still waters. This is not God's promise; it is not our experience; it is not that simple. My gleaming Gateway Arch, which I can so easily romanticize, does not mean the same thing to the Native American peoples who lost their cherished lands and way of life to western settlement. Doors through which we pass can mark the beginning of grief and pain beyond our imagination, and we are fools if we do not avoid them when we can. But avoiding gateways simply because they are the entrance to unfamiliar and uncomfortable territory is a deathly habit. If we only labor to stay where we are or return to where we have been, we will shrivel up and die.

Yes, if we are sane we tremble before gateways. Yet God's word to us is not the superficially safe one. God does not say, "Stay out of gateways; they are dangerous places." God's promise rather is: "The gates of hell will not prevail. Move on and ahead. I will go before you, and I will be with you. I will keep your going out and your coming in from this time forth forevermore. Life in my reign will be more abundant than you can imagine." God stands at the gateways of our lives, particularly those that are shaped like a cross.

There is a remaining thing for us as a church to say about the figure of the good shepherd. It is crucial to realize that the Good Shepherd among us is not our pastor or any of our clergy. We all too frequently err in identifying them that way, expecting them to be more than they are intended to be. In doing so we set ourselves up for disillusionment, we set them up to burn out and fail, and we both become angry. Of course many clergy collude in this----who would not like to be called good shepherds, like God among their people?

But the Good Shepherd is always God. The religious leaders among us are to point away from themselves and toward this truth----nothing more, nothing less. It is in this recognition of our dependence on God that we discover the paradox always at the heart of profound truth: as we acknowledge we are sheep among sheep before God, we can become shepherds to each other. As sheep before God, we can be shepherds in the church and to the world.

When Jesus describes himself as the good shepherd, he is describing the church. When Jesus says, "I am the good shepherd," he is telling us how we are to be:

> We are to bring the thirsty to refreshment, to the water that quenches all longing and washes parched throats and aching hands and feet.

> We are to stand up to the false shepherds, those who scatter, rob, and kill.

> We are to search out those who are lost and without hope, knowing how easy it is to wander away alone.

> We are to dare to place ourselves in gateways, so we and others can move through them in safety to the future God intends.

Second Movement

BAPTISM
AND COMMUNITY

All praise and thanks to you, most merciful Father,
for adopting us as your own children,
for incorporating us into your holy Church,
and for making us worthy to share in the inheritance
of the saints in light.

The Company of Christ

---- We receive you into the household of God. ----

ONCE WE HAVE DISCOVERED the richness and value of community, as I did as a child in the warm circle of my grandmother's Methodist friends, we will know what to seek. We will ask: "Can I join the followers of Jesus, or am I to be alone? Will they let me lean against them when the way becomes hard? Will they lean against me?" We will seek a company in which formative stories can be heard and holy habits can be practiced, and we will know it when we find it.

One way we find it is through the sacrament of baptism. We become members of God's household, the company of those who follow Jesus and who take God's story—and all of its astonishing implications—to the other households of the world. As members of this household we need never be alone again. We will have the shoulders of saints against which to lean. And we can be broad-shouldered saints as well.

But many of us have great difficulty in seeing ourselves as members of companies, of communities, as being in continuing relationship with each other. Instead, we have been brought up to see ourselves as individuals, with legalistic claims to what we call our "rights." Even with Paul's rich legacy to us regarding the nature of this one, holy, catholic, and apostolic body, we too often ignore the truth of our being that community uniquely called together to restore all people to unity with God and each other in Christ. The children in our midst can feel alone indeed.

I have found some help with this difficulty from my early training as a biologist in college and graduate school. I had the intention of spending my professional life in a research laboratory. Fortunately, I discovered early on that this was not who I was and what I was to do, and gradually I found my way into my current work —teaching, writing, and consulting in the church. Nevertheless, I consider that early training as critical for who I am and what I do. It left me with a deep love for God's natural order, and it gave me an inherent understanding of living systems. Thus I see our human communities—including the church—in shades of green, not in black and white, For me, their analogue is more a growing tree than an expanding organizational chart or a machine—even my friendly computer!

I know from my work in the church, informed by my work in the laboratory, that such systems are not static or easily grasped, but messy and mysterious companies of persons. Thus they hold both surprise and promise for us. Finally, we cannot control them; we can only view them with awe and humility. Nonetheless, living systems do have certain characteristics, and respectful exploration of these can offer insight to render our work richer, more purposeful, more faithful. Further, use of the words "community" or "body" in the place of "living system" may make these characteristics more apropos to that remarkable system which is the church. A beginning definition of such a body is: *two or more living parts related to each other in order to carry out a particular purpose.*

Such bodies *have skins or boundaries that separate the inside from the outside.* This is the defining characteristic, for without a skin our bodies would fly apart and would no longer exist—our molecules would float around with all other molecules in the environment, and we would no longer have our own peculiar identity.

When we describe a particular body or community, we usually begin with physical location and facility: "Our church is the red brick building on the corner of North Avenue and First Street." "We are a small frame church on the outskirts of town, the one with the steeple." Moreover, the boundary of a community—whether it is a congregation, a school, or a family—also includes a unique story that no one else can tell: the past and present that belong to them alone, future dreams that light the way before them. The defining skin includes the rules and values by which life is ordered, and it involves the question of belonging.

To say we will welcome all who come to our door is different from saying that all who come to our door become part of the family. These newcomers need to know who we are and for what we stand before they and we make decisions about membership. Being inclusive does not mean saying that anything goes. "What does it mean to belong here? What will you expect of me? What can I expect of you?" are crucial boundary questions. Such are the questions we ask and answer every time someone is baptized into the body of Christ, every time we renew our own baptismal covenant:

> *Will you...?*
> *I will, with God's help.*

I know of a parish that is very clear about their standards and expectations for membership: members tithe, and they practice a rule of daily prayer and service to the community. While the number of those who "officially" belong to this congregation is not extremely large and remains rather steady, the number of those who affiliate has swelled over time. These affiliates are people who need a community of dependability and constancy that they can trust in times when all else around them is shaking and slipping. They know that they will be tended to faithfully by such people. They sojourn for a while and then leave to go on with their lives, strengthened by a rock-solid adherence to boundaries.

Vital bodies understand that *every one of their parts is connected to every other part, and each part is dependent on all the others for the completion of the whole.* Indeed, it is this connectedness of the various members that gives living systems their characteristic qualities: they are always more than the sum of their parts. Paul said it well in his first letter to the church in Corinth:

> If the whole body were an eye, where would the hearing be? If the whole body were hearing, where would the sense of smell be? But as it is, God arranged the members in the body, each one of them, as he chose. If all were a single member, where would the body be? As it is, there are many members, yet one body. (1 Corinthians 12:17-20)

Small changes anywhere affect the whole. A lift in spirit gives spring to the step; a dull ache in the shoulder permeates the spine. What happens here influences what is going on there, even if that effect is imperceptible at the time. This means that we compartmentalize and isolate to our peril. Such efforts ultimately are futile; our sense of separateness finally is delusion. This means that every voice is to be heard, even the small and faint one that can be speaking truth for the whole. This means that any person's entering or leaving the circle on the porch changes that circle into a different one. This means that we are to begin working wherever we find opening and receptivity, for that work will spread throughout the body.

The community is healthy only when the differing contributions of the various members are recognized, valued, and encouraged. We are called to welcome the healthy tension of heterogeneity—diversity—without which creativity cannot emerge. And when we consider the boundaries flung around the larger communities of church, nation, world, and indeed all of creation, we must acknowledge the connections among all that God has made. Any notion of our being independent and self-sufficient is folly.

I am encouraged by the growing number of communities that are becoming aware of their relationship to all others. What and how much they buy, how they order time, how long and when they burn lights, how they dispose of wastes, even on what kind of plates they serve food and from what kind of containers they drink coffee, are not their business alone. All of our habits, holy and otherwise, affect the health of the whole earth.

Healthy bodies—communities—are *in constant tension regarding change.* If we are alive we are always changing; we become different from one moment to the next, even if that difference is imperceptible—as when we shed hair or replace the cells of our skin. We anticipate and respond to influences from our surroundings; we anticipate and respond to activity within our own skins. We shift and stir and shrink and spread; we soar and sink. We know that stagnation and status quo only result in death—in fact, they define death. We adapt, or we perish.

However, healthy bodies also expend considerable energy in resisting change. And we are wise to do so, for we know that life will be different in the wake of meta-morphosis. Transformation is risky business indeed. The butterfly in all its graceful flight will no longer be able to crawl across sweet-smelling ground. Further, we know that unbridled change also results in a deathly fly-ing apart at the seams, in a dissolution of vital order. Yet our all-too-frequent error is to see those parts of the body that speak for the status quo as reactionary and backward. Continuity and adaptation are not mutually exclusive; indeed, they both are part and parcel of con-stant transformation and hearty growth.

I know of a congregation that is contemplating selling their building and buying another in order to accommo-date rapid growth. Realizing what a wrenching change this move would be to members, they have put together a study committee made up of those who are excited about the prospects of the move and those who think it would be a terrible mistake. These people are working together on the implications of staying on the current property or leaving it, and have planned a weekend event to hear from all the voices in the congregation—even the children. They know that a sound decision can only come from respectful dialogue.

Sound bodies are aware of *the cyclical nature of their lives.* We know that we are ever being born or maturing or stabilizing or waning or dying or being resurrected, again whether these movements are clearly perceptible in the moment or not. We are to welcome each move-ment as normal and predictable rather than as a dreaded anomaly. Each movement has its own graceful rhythm; each offers its own opportunity for response. We are not finally in control of God's successions. Our responsibil-ity is to participate faithfully in them.

Parts of the body also move through their own cycles as well. Just as a healthy person does not resist putting on glasses when eye muscles become weaker with time, vigorous and healthy communities know that continuing in "blindness" is foolish vanity. We must allow worn-out practices to die so that new habits can be born. A vital community knows that death precedes life, that transformation means the passing of old ways. The community that has been drowned in the waters of baptism is one that can live boldly into new life.

I know of a small mission congregation that is coming into being in the mountains of North Georgia. They are asking questions regarding beginnings, for they are aware that they are developing new habits that will become tradition all too soon. They know they have a chance to develop *holy* habits right from the start, and they want their "but-we-have-always-done-it-this-way"'s to reflect faithful worship and sound stewardship. For example, they all have committed to tithe. These people are not waiting to become better established and stronger before they find and carry out their ministry within the surrounding community. They are struggling with identifying this ministry even as they are emerging as a community themselves.

One final characteristic of living systems is critical to our understanding of life in community, in the company of disciples: every living body *exists for a purpose that provides its driving energy*. We included this purpose in our opening definition of such systems. However, it deserves special emphasis, for neglect in naming and proclaiming this aim is suicidal. Communities that do not or cannot demonstrate clarity of purpose—literally a *raison d'être*—drift and sputter and die. They do not have the breath necessary for life. And companies without purpose are not attractive to the outsider. They cannot offer an inviting circle of chairs, or cake that is moist and tea that is minty and ice cold.

I have heard the story of an inner-city parish whose numbers had steadily decreased and whose membership had grown increasingly older over the years. No longer needing space for educational programs and the like, they gave their facility over for use by various community agencies. Then came the bad news: they needed to replace the entire roof. They discussed moving to the suburbs, where new members might be found, but decided instead to put on the finest roof money could buy. Later someone asked the local bag lady about that congregation. She said she did not know any of them personally but she was grateful for them: "They give me hope. Everyone else is leaving the city, but they are staying. They just built a new roof!"

We must heed two notes of warning, though. Clarity about aim does not mean that that aim is in concert with the reign of God. Demonic systems can produce great energy for survival and growth. Moreover, that which we espouse as purpose or mission and what we actually practice are never in absolute harmony. Indeed, they can be quite far apart. Our need to survive as a body always pollutes our practice to some degree. So we are to ask continually, "What do we intend, and what is actually happening?"

Further, whether we are always aware of it or not, we are members of numerous bodies and communities that are in constant relationship and tension with each other. We can be confused and dismayed by their conflicting purposes and demands when we do not identify the ultimate boundary or skin as the one circumscribing God's reign. We are in relationship with the entire creation by virtue of our common foundation in God. Our mission is the healing and reconciliation of God's creation. All other purposes are to be held up against this plumb line, the one that is straight and true.

Bones

— Will you persevere in resisting evil, and, whenever you fall
into sin, repent and return to the Lord? —

THE BODY THAT LOSES ITS SKIN *will die. The body that
does not adapt and change when the world changes overnight will perish, as will the one that does not attend to
the seasons of its days. The body that is not nourished by
the blood of connection will grow thin. The body that is
not grounded in faithful relationship to God will be re-
duced to nothing but a collection of dusty and dead
bones.*

*Ezekiel, God's prophet to the exiled people of Israel in
Babylon, walks in a dusty field of disconnected bones
that once moved together to Jerusalem's song of life----foot
bones, leg bones, backbones, arm bones, shoulder bones,
head bones. Now their bleak stirrings are directed by the
dry-blowing wind. Their song is a rattling, clattering,
chattering chorus of death. The prophet shudders with the
shaking bones. "Why has God dropped me in this field of
despair? The wind dries my mouth and shrivels my
flesh."*

*Ezekiel's words do not speak to us. We see ourselves
among the privileged. We dance circling steps of certainty. We gaze on fertile fields of achievement. Our
tongues are moist with confidence. We are plump with the
nourishment of success.*

*God says to the prophet, "Look at the deathly sticks;
see them." And the parching wind sears his soul. And*

God asks the prophet, "Can these bones live?" And the prophet answers, "Only you know."

Then God utters strange words to the prophet. God says: "The rattle of bones must now come before a dance of life. And only those who acknowledge their deathly disobedience----those who shake with the clacking bones---- can hope to call forth my breath from the wind and live again." Hear the word of the Lord.

We cannot live long in the fallacy of assumed favor. We must feel the drying wind whistling through the remains of our lifeless illusions. We must walk amidst the disconnected bones lying in our dusty fields of self-interest:

Bones of pride, forgetting that all we have and are comes from God, claiming honor for ourselves.

Bones of greed, desiring for ourselves what belongs to all others, not heeding our relationship with them.

Bones of avarice, longing to possess more and more while those around us have less and less.

Bones of sloth, neglecting to care for sky and field, the children in our midst, and the beggar at our gate.

Bones of gluttony, satiating ourselves with the tea and cake of our feasts while others have no meal at all.

Bones of lust, seeing the issue of divine labor as objects to satisfy our appetites rather than sisters and brothers born of God.

Bones of anger, nursing our resentments into the

dark of our nights, hanging on and on to irritation and hostility.

God provides the view of the disconnected bones, places us squarely in the field we seek to avoid. The dust blows in our teeth, soils our clothes, and stings our eyes.

God asks, "Can these bones live?" And we are to respond in faith, "Only you know." Then God will speak the strange words of grace to us. God will say, "The rattle of bones precedes the dance of life." And God will continue, "Prophesy to the bones; say to them, 'O dry bones, hear the word of the Lord.'"

And the bones will clatter no more. They will take on sinew, flesh, and skin. They will join together and whirl in joy. God's ever-present wind will continue to blow, but it will no longer parch, no longer singe and shrivel. It will be heavy with fresh rains of prospect.

God's prophet to Israel walks in the valley of the bones. He hears the voice of God to the people of God; he speaks God's word of life. He summons God's breath from the wind, and God's people arise in power.

We too can be God's prophets in the valley of the bones. We are to face the bones. We are to hear and to speak God's words. If we but will, those bones will take on sinew, flesh, and skin. They will dance. God's people will breathe the fresh wind of hope. They will dream of possibility. They will stand on their feet, "a vast multitude."

"I have spoken," says the Lord. "Amen," we sing and sing.

Navigation

— Now sanctify this water,...that those who here are cleansed from sin and born again may continue for ever in the risen life of Jesus Christ our Savior. —

YEARS AGO A SAILOR FRIEND gave me an important piece of information: three navigational points are required if one is to chart a course, if one intends to set direction with confidence and purpose. "You need to know where you are now and from where you set sail if you are ever to reach some intended point on your chart," he explained. I knew he was talking about stars and banks of islands, but his instruction has become an important metaphor for my understanding of the human journey. If we are to set out in the hope of reaching our destination----the future God intends for us----we will need to reflect on two other points: our past as we remember it and our present as we name it.

Charting a course from this perspective means that we again and again are to hear and to tell the story that is ours alone----the story that has shaped our identity, our skin; the story that tells us who we have been so we can know both who we are and who we can be. What we have done in the past influences both the actions we take today and our accomplishments of tomorrow. Where we have been influences where we are and where we will go. Our histories are connected to our dreams. Remember, the child on the porch was set on her way by the tales of the good Methodist women.

Charting a course from this perspective also necessitates our seeing the current moment with clear and unwavering eyes. It provides us with a measure of reality: this is how it is or at least how it seems to be for now. We are to identify the pressures and demands bombarding us from all sides, and we are to listen and look for words and signs of support and encouragement that will enable us to move ahead. The child on the porch observed everything around her and took it all in, and she learned of habit and community and character.

When I think about the image of these three metaphorical navigational points, one parish always comes to my mind. It is a rural Episcopal church in the Southeast with a history of conflict, and when the senior warden called me, he described the congregation as stalled, "a ship dead in the water." There was something about his sense of discouragement and fatigue, coupled with an obvious devotion to the church and a commitment to its work, that caught and held me.

The following story is not about that parish per se, but about the work of any group of people at a difficult time in their communal life---people who represent all of us who care about the church and at the same time are discontented with the quality of life within its walls. It is a story about the work of the people of God, about the importance of our taking time apart to be in the presence of God and each other, an unexceptional story about ordinary people.

We began on a Friday evening with the telling of personal stories about life in the parish. "What brought us to this church? Can we recall and describe significant times or events? What keeps us here; what holds us?": these were the questions around which we shaped the conversation. Words came slowly at first; the parishioners were not in the habit of talking to each other. Then there was *laughter as they relived awkward moments, and a few shed tears as they revisited painful times. In retrospect, none of the stories recounted was notable, though each was important for the teller to tell. We heard of births, marriages, illnesses, and deaths; of parties and funerals; of Christmases and Easters: the substance of their lives in that place. They spoke of the significance of that community for them over the years and named some of the ingredients of the glue that held them together: warmth, support, nourishment, company----the altar, the bread and the wine. Again and again someone murmured, "I could not have gotten through it without all of you." I felt the stirring of the child as she listened to the tales of the good Methodist ladies so many years ago.*

We continued the next morning with stories of the history of the community. Their task was to ask of that history: "What kind of people are we? We are a people who...? For what and for whom do we stand?" They were to uncover the values imparted by the past----for better and for worse: the legacy that both facilitated and impeded steps forward. The ensuing discussion was lively; the residues of anxiety and reticence from the night before faded further. Once again, the accounts were not particularly memorable, but they began to paint the picture of a tenacious people who had faced dry times before, when membership declined and the resources to make necessary repairs on their building just were not there, when any thoughts of money for special music or supplies or refreshments were in vain. "But we made it, didn't we? We're still here. We are survivors!" They had come through desert wilderness before, and they could do so again. Confidence and energy swelled, and I suspected that they had begun to cast glances toward the future.

We spent Saturday afternoon looking at the present: "This is the way it is----or seems to be for now." The local economy based on farming and light manufacturing was sagging; members of the congregation had been laid off from work. Children were leaving the community for jobs in the city. The rector was sixty years old; his health was tentative, but he was physically able to stay on until retirement and had nowhere else to go. Then as they looked these realities straight in the eye, they also began to explore needs of the neighborhood and town. They began to define the "successful" church as one that engages with the larger community in which it is located, not necessarily one that is growing in numbers or programs. They began to talk of their responsibility to carry the gospel of life and hope into the world beyond their immediate boundaries. After all, they were were not the only ones whose livelihoods were threatened, the only ones with disappearing children and diminishing health. Words came quickly and with growing energy.

Saturday evening's session began with a heated confrontation between the rector and parishioners regarding issues of mutual accountability. One man said, "We've stopped walking on tiptoes, and I'm glad!" Members of the vestry began to see the necessity of their assuming their responsibilities as leaders of the congregation; the rector could not and should not go it alone. After this discussion----or because of it----they moved on to envision the future, working in small groups: "What would we like to see going on here in three to five years?" I reminded them to consider the lessons of their past story. I suggested they call on their imaginations and not dwell on the confines of the present: willingness to engage in future dreaming provides the energy for fresh possibility. They decided to wait for the light of the morning's day to unveil their efforts.

We closed with the service of Compline. As people drifted away in twos and threes, the rector and I sat down together for a brief talk. He was relieved that there would be some shifting of the load from his shoulders. He was grateful that he would have a place to be until he could retire, but he was painfully aware of the cost to the parish of his continuing to serve as their ordained leader. I did not sleep well that night.

The pictures of the future revealed at the closing session on Sunday morning were modest in scope, generally focused around themes of commitment, community, communication, and education. But these people at least could now assume a future. Then, with no apparent warning, they plunged into another heated conversation----this time about the nature of the Eucharist. They questioned their daring to approach the altar when at odds with a sister or brother. I suspected several had the rector in mind. Questions became clearer than answers, and the wrestling was fierce. Implicit in this discussion seemed to be an awareness that, while they had a measure of new hope and some fresh sense of confidence with which to move into the future, the realities of their predicament had not disappeared. The road ahead might be walkable, but the traveling would be difficult and uncertain. They worked in small groups for the last time, clarifying next steps as specifically as possible.

The closing Eucharist was poignant. We had remained at our places in the conference room. For the Eucharistic Prayer we stood at our chairs and faced each other across the circle of tables. But as the rector began to administer the bread and wine among us, we turned outward in order to receive communion. We now were facing away from the tables with our backs to each other! I saw this as an unconscious but visible sign of continuing distress.

I talked to the senior warden briefly before we left. He said Saturday had been a low day for him. For the first time in his long history with this congregation he could not clearly answer the question, "Why do I remain?" But he said that he knew he would remain—because there was nowhere else for him to go. The church may be imperfect in its living of and witnessing to Christ's gospel, but there was no other body that could offer a satisfying alternative.

The drive home was a low time for me as I struggled with the same question: Why do I remain? And this senior warden's answer is mine as well: There is nowhere else to go. More positively expressed, the church alone promises the possibility of God's transforming power for change. On the road home I also experienced a sense of gratitude for my time in the midst of courageous men and women who had lived into their pain and who had come away with a measure of renewed hope. There were no good or bad people there, just real people involved in the mess and mystery of death and life, of sin and of grace.

The navigational metaphor that informed the weekend continues to take shape and afford guidance for my understanding of the human journey. Through the poetry of the prophet Isaiah God says to me:

> "Cease your dwelling in long-ago days and your brooding on stale stories. Here and now I make it possible for you to set forth on a new course, to set sail toward a new day; do you not perceive it? Lift up your eyes; look around you; search the horizon: what do you see that you've never seen before? Tune your ears to the song of the heavens: what strains do you hear for the very first time?

> "The signs are all there. You are not to be bound by where you have been. Your direction is not predetermined, nor are you confined by today's winds. But it only will be possible for you to em-

bark on this journey——one beyond your imagin-
ing——if you cease your attempts to control and be-
gin trusting in me. Only then can you receive the
fresh breezes of the Spirit's power and point into
the future that is mine alone."

Power and Authority

---- Teach them to love others in the power of the Spirit. ----

OUR LIFE AND WORK within communities, for good or ill, is directed by the power we perceive ourselves to have, or others perceive us to have. A beginning definition of power is the ability to exercise influence. When we ask about our power, we are asking whether or not others will listen to us; we are questioning whether or not we can sway and persuade. When as a child I wondered if I might tell my own story in the gathered company on my grandmother's porch, I was beginning to examine my power.

Several years ago I attended a conference that brought together a group of people committed to the social activist ministries—those efforts that involve work among the suffering and needy, whether by providing immediate relief or striving for systemic change. My job that week was to observe and listen, and then to write a report. As I moved from room to room, the word I entered again and again in my notebook was "power."

The people there spoke of power in a variety of ways. They talked of gathering power and empowering others and of having no power at all, of being powerless. I could not always find common understanding among them, and some admitted that they were uncomfortable dealing with power in the first place: they thought of it in a negative way. Further, they either made little reference to authority, or they used the words "power" and "authority" interchangeably. In compiling my observations, I began my own work of sorting and defining.

Beginning with the creation narratives, the biblical story tells us that the source of all power is God. Power can be described metaphorically as the energy breathed by God into creation. Indeed, the Greek word frequently translated as "power" in the New Testament is *dunamis*, from which we receive words like "dynamite" and "dynamic." All people have inherent power by virtue of their creation by God, of their being alive. Whether or not we choose to use our power becomes the critical question for each of us. Denial of that power—both because of and in spite of our varying circumstances—is a denial of God's gift of life. Our claims of powerlessness are occasions of being unfaithful.

For Christians the story goes on. In baptism, those already created with the power of God flowing in their veins now receive the power of the Holy Spirit in their hearts. They are grafted into the eternal priesthood of the crucified and resurrected Christ, a royal people ordained to serve the world. Power upon power—a heady combination until we remember that power now is defined by suffering love, by the death of God on the cross.

But while saying that all persons have God-given power provides a theological foundation for us, it would be naive to leave the statement there. We would not be providing a responsible answer, for there are factors, such as institutional or community position and social status, that enhance or diminish the power we have in a particular body or community. The chairman of the board has more power—the ability to exercise influence—than does a member of the typing pool; a member of a founding family has more influence in certain communities than a new arrival. I recently was told by someone in a very old congregation, "We really are newcomers here and don't have much influence; we've only lived in this city for twenty-five years."

Resources—wealth, education, technology—are factors that affect our potency. People who are adept in the computer sciences increasingly hold power that can supersede the influence of their position in the organizational chart. Genetic constitution—sex, race, stature, energy—provide currencies of power in particular circumstances. Being a woman or a man, being black or white, being young or old, or being short or tall present obstacles in some paths but advantages in others.

Access to and means of distributing information are valuable commodities of power—always well used by effective community organizers. "Who knows what's going on, and how is the word spread?" The retired woman on the block is a powerhouse of communication because she has time to know everyone in the neighborhood, and she is trusted. Reputation and power are always closely connected.

In itself, each of these factors is neutral. It can be used to enhance the power of others, or when separated from its source—God—it can be used to bind and to oppress. Some are valued more highly in one community than in another, so each community must be evaluated in its own right. And those of us who possess valued currencies of power—resources, education, and the like—in larger measure than others are called to use them toward the end that all God's people will come to have their share. Paradoxically, the more power is shared, the more abundant it becomes for all. Power is not a limited commodity, for God continues to breathe into our midst.

Years ago a colleague and I were in competition with each other. (Competition—even the healthy variety—is ultimately about power.) She and I, two women getting started in the system, believed that there was just not enough work, attention, and praise for both of us, so we were constantly jockeying for position and pushing the other aside with not-so-subtle verbal nudges. The whole business became increasingly wearying and unpleasant for us both, and for the others around us.

Eventually, I mustered the courage to have a talk with her about our behavior, and we promised each other that we would try to act differently. The results were amazing. Instead of competing, we now were supporting. Both of us became happier and more relaxed. Both of us received generous commendation and opportunities for advancement. In other words, we both had more power once we were able to put our greed for power aside.

Legitimate power is always shared power; it allows others their influence as well. God's own use of power provides the model for us. God does not coerce or manipulate. God does not appropriate. God has given us power and has not taken away our freedom to decide how we will exercise it. Claims to power that deny the right of others to use their God-given power become sinful distortions and denials of the power of God.

So rather than declare ourselves powerless in the face of the complex world we are called upon to serve, the critical question becomes: "What bases of power *do* we have in this situation, and how can we employ them most faithfully and effectively?" Further, we are to ask: "What bases of power do those we are here to serve have, and how can we help them use and enhance their own power?" Or, "How can we and these others best symbolize the breath of God—the *dunamis*—in the communities and circumstances in which we find ourselves?" After all, we have been received into the household of God; we have been anointed and reborn by the power of the Holy Spirit in baptism.

However, deciding to use our power legitimately involves resolving the issue of authority. One understanding of authority is having the right and therefore the responsibility to use power. The questions now become: "Do we have the *right* to use the power we indeed have, and if so, what gives us that right?" Again, the ultimate source of our authority is God. The Greek word frequently translated as "authority" in the New Testament is *exousia*, "out of being": we have the right to be and to do because God planted it within us from the beginning. But this means that all other persons have the right to be and to do as well. I may have the power—the ability—to speak certain words, but if they are words that hurt you or diminish your freedom to speak, then I do not have the right to speak them.

Further, we must realize that we can exercise power not because of our claim to God-given authority, but because people will pay attention to us and will be open to our influence. Others finally grant us the authority to use our power. Again, there are enhancing factors, each valued to a greater or lesser degree in a given body. While institutional or community position—rector, principal, chief executive officer, mother, father—is frequently the initial source of one's authority, it cannot stand alone. Taken by itself, it will become fragile and illegitimate.

Other factors for consideration can include personal charisma, our education, and the wisdom we are perceived to possess. However, it is our reputation—others' history of experience with us—that is most important. Our reputation involves our authenticity, consistency, competency, and dependability demonstrated over time. It involves our faithful pursuit of the mission or purpose of the community. It has to do with spirituality and moral example. Reputation concerns character, those dispositions to behave in certain ways. It is the aggregate of the stories people tell about us—and to which the child listens. In other words, people will grant us authority to the degree that they trust us.

Our separate claims to power and authority will inevitably come into conflict as we strive to live together in community—even when that community is the company of Christ! When this happens, we are to be open to each other—especially to those with whom we disagree. We are to acknowledge our dependence upon them for a perspective we cannot glean by ourselves. As we can hold fast to the reality of our connectedness, we will be more able to give and receive the blessings God intends for us all.

The Sea

— We thank you, Almighty God, for the gift of water. Over
it the Holy Spirit moved in the beginning of creation. —

*EVERY YEAR SINCE I WAS A SMALL CHILD I have gone to
the sea, and I have seen the drama of redemption played
out as if for the first time. Long before I knew the biblical
story, I saw in the sea's movements the ancient battle between the mysterious powers of creation and destruction,
the power of God and the power of evil. As they rolled
and churned together in the deep, the two combatants
were sometimes difficult to distinguish.*

*Even as a child I sensed the issue at stake to be the
fundamental one: Would life prevail, or would death's
darkness speak the last word? It was as if the battle for
my soul were being waged: Would my internal chaos
wash over and drown all in me that yearned for life and
expression, or would those yearnings be allowed to germi-
nate and come to fruition? I watched in dread and fasci-
nation, and year after year, I found my answer in the
movement of the tide. In its predictability a sense of
something on which to depend began to emerge from the
roar.*

*I could mark time by the tide. On quiet days the insis-
tent water regularly crept to the line it had left before.
Then with a playful turn it frolicked away to leave behind the widest beach, rife with the signs of the lush life
sustained in the depths of the sea. In storms it pounded
in, but still it came, and still it turned. Order was evi-*

dent in the tide, the harmony God's power brings to chaos and disruption. It is this harmony that distinguishes God's nourishing power from the frenzied and alluring power of evil, the power that separates and tears in its surges. Even as a child I saw in the sea's movements the victory of life over death.

The sea's lessons have expanded for me over the years. They have taught me about rhythm, the give and take inherent in the created order. And the sea's storms have shaken my complacency, my willingness to accept too much order or a cheap order that does not emerge from struggle. The sea has come to represent all I cannot control, cannot manipulate for good or for ill; it does as it wills. I have learned to survive in the sea; I know I must submit to it, swim with it, or I will drown. Yet I have been bathed and cleansed in my deepest places by those sea waters, better able to face the grime and beauty of the streets I will travel after I leave it behind for another season.

The sea has come to represent the way things are—those truths that are prerequisites for life and health. It has come to symbolize those things about which I can do nothing, of which I must let go. The sea stands for power I cannot fathom, power that brings forth life and cares for it, power greater than my own. As a child and as an adult I have named that power God and have been comforted and strengthened in so doing.

One year my drive to the sea did not include a lightening of my spirit. It took me past row after row of burned corn limply standing in dusty brown powder. The Southeast was suffering its worst drought in decades, and these fields were grim evidence of the killer stalking the livelihood of anyone who depended on the steady availability of water. During those summer months, weeks had gone by with soaring temperatures and with either no rainfall or teasing showers the ground did not notice----a sprinkle of tears, a cruel reminder of what should be.

I did not leave the tragedy behind when I arrived at the sea. Night after night the nation joined me in watching newscasts of brown death overtaking generations of dreams and toil. We saw countless scenes of dead chickens and starving cattle and haggard, hopeless faces of men and women----studies in powerlessness and futility. We saw wordless prayers hurled into the empty hot sky----angry, honest prayers that likely strayed close to blasphemy. This devastation confronting me every evening was an ironic contrast to the endless expanse of water stretching before me during the day, and as I plodded back and forth through the blistering sand between them, the sea seemed to me to lose its power to give life. Although intellectually I understood that it held only a piece of the meteorological puzzle, its movements in and out became a mocking motion. A suspicion of powerlessness----mine and God's----began to settle into my bones.

Then another story unfolded on the television screen. Airplanes and trucks loaded with hay from the Midwest and New England were arriving in southern airports and towns. Farmers who could tell their own stories of brushes with ruin were responding. Their gifts were accompanied by an element of risk, for they might need the hay themselves in the months to come. And they were not fooling themselves; they could not send what finally was needed. If rain did not fall soon, what they gave would mean little. But they also understood that their moist earth touched the cracked southern ground, and they could not ignore the implications. What those farmers could not know was that their gifts fed more than starving cattle and wilting hope. They spoke to the shriveling spirit of one who sat by the sea and who lives in a city. My yearly healing from the sea could begin.

From my experiences at the sea's side, I have been helped to distinguish between the concepts of power and authority. Power can be understood as the energy breathed by God into creation. It is our heartbeat and the heartbeat of the universe. It is the surging of the sea. The right or the responsibility----the authority----to use this power comes from God as well. The sea powerfully rolls with its God-given permission to do so; those distant farmers acted with the same right. Just as the sea has freedom to caress or pound, they had the power to bring hay to the South or to withhold it. They responded out of their sense of responsibility----of authority. They responded out of their sense of rightful power----of God-given power.

God-given power appreciates connectedness. *It is always concerned with the relational and open to that which it cannot know. The men and women in the Midwest and New England sensed that their land did not exist separately from land in other parts of the country, even though they may never have seen the Georgia plain or the rolling hills of the Carolina countryside. And they certainly never guessed that their actions were connected to those of a woman sitting in gloom by the side of the sea. We can boldly extrapolate and say that our concerns are mysteriously linked to everyone and everything everywhere. Sea waters lap every shore.*

God-given power recognizes responsibility. *As we understand ourselves in relationship to all others, we can do nothing less than engage with them and give. We can no longer live lives of isolation; we have no right to live as if no one or nothing else exists. The farmers gave when it might have made no difference, knowing that what we do, what we eat, what and how much we buy have far-reaching effects. Our decisions cannot be made blindly, without attention to their consequences. The sea is not* rational and moral, yet the consequences of its actions are felt by those who live at its boundaries. When we are not sensitive to the effects of our cutting down and our building up, we are not responsible to the order of the creation of which we are a part.

Power used with God-given authority honors limits. This was one of the earliest lessons from my teacher, the sea. I saw the sea move in to the land, engage with it, nuzzle and play with it, even slap it, and then in the turn of the tide recognize the land's own right to exist. The farmers could send hay, but they could not bring rain, nor could they take over the cares of their brothers and sisters to the south. In our mutual touches we help define each other, but finally we must acknowledge that we are different, that we have our own right to be and our own work to do.

Further, as distinct authorities we will conflict with each other. However, this conflict is the genesis of our separate and unique contributions to the creative process. To engage in struggle----to keep coming back and sorting out in our pursuit of God's will----is the truest expression of our own authority and our recognition of its limits. It is well to remember that even God chooses to use holy power within rightful bounds.

The Creator has always remained connected to creation. The moist ground of heaven touches the cracked soil of earth. This conjunction marks the story of God's relationship to humankind and to all else fashioned by the divine hand. And God never lets go. God pursues; God badgers; God loves----even when we do all in our power to sever the connection. The biblical story tells us that nothing can cut us loose. God will keep coming back to remind us of whose we are and who we are created to be. Our fundamental connection to each other is established in this persistent relationship of God with all that God has made.

God hears and responds to the creation's cries, and Jesus Christ is the absolute revelation of that response. God could do nothing less than enter the scene in the flesh, engage with humankind as one of us, and live as God intends for us to live. In Jesus' responses to those who were hurting, sick, oppressed, hungry and thirsty for the food and water that would relieve for all time, we are given the pattern of how we are to respond to each other. In the person of Jesus we have power and authority held in their perfect tension. That is why he amazed and astounded those around him and why he was so offensive to those in self-serving power. Jesus constantly sorted and chose among the myriad authorities before him----as we must do----and the right to say what he said and do what he did came from the highest source.

But we prefer not to maintain the tension between power and authority, for living in tension is difficult. We prefer to keep power and authority estranged, for then we can ignore relationships----of person to person, church to larger world, business to church, nation to nation. We do not have to take into account the authority of all those others made in God's image as well. But separation from each other offends and dishonors the one whose likeness we carry----the God who is connected to us by choice, who seeks relationship with us and responds to us even in our sin.

God does not force the divine power on us because even God does not have the right----by God's own choice----to disregard our freedom. God wills to leave the power of evil alive in creation, and we must choose between that and divine power. God invites us to join the process of creation, but we are free to spurn the invitation. When our efforts are wrenched from God's purpose and we ignore the limits imposed by others' authority, those efforts become tragically torn and disfigured. The power coursing through our bodies and our hearts is God's power. We have the right to use it because of who we are----God's people----and God has given that authority to us. Power used with appropriate authority furthers God's reign of peace and justice, bringing order and life. This is always the test. Power not grounded in the divine source is power seized without God-given authority. Power used for our own purposes alone brings disharmony and separation, and they are synonymous with sin.

God came to us as an outsider to the power structures of the world. God gave up control to these powers and hung on the cross. If we live as God intends, we too will be outsiders, and we will suffer. But the nature of God's power was perfectly demonstrated on that same cross. Only from such apparent powerlessness does life-giving power emerge: power that takes seriously the effects of our sin and our separation, and the reality of death. Power that is victorious over everything we can do to deny it.

Preacher Man

— Will you seek and serve Christ in all persons,
loving your neighbor as yourself? —

IT WAS THE LAST DAY OF APRIL. *I was sitting on the front
steps of the Episcopal Center's Peachtree Road entrance
during my lunch hour, soaking in the warmth of the early
spring sun. I caught sight of a man walking down the ad-
jacent horseshoe driveway. I looked the other way up into
the traffic and hoped he would not approach. I did not
want my reverie spoiled. I did not want to respond to him
or to anyone else at the moment. But of course he did, as
I knew he would, and he introduced himself as a preacher
of the gospel.*

*He was an old man, toothless, and with the cloudy,
hazy eyes of age. Spit flew as he talked. He wore a jaunty
French fisherman's cap and a green jacket with a torn
sleeve, and he carried a gray Adidas bag. I could understand about half of what he said.*

*"Up the street at that other church they told me they
couldn't give money. That's not true. They could. They
don't want to. We can do what we want to do." I nodded
in agreement, aware of a tightening in my gut.*

*"I'm not talking about religion, you know. Religion is
just an obligation to do your duty. Those people who come
to church every Sunday but who don't live any different
are religious people." More tightening. I was washed with
the spray of his words.*

"You can't get to God without having to deal with me first. Can't do it." I recalled that the gospel lesson for the day was from the fourteenth chapter of John: *"I am the way."* I felt fear and a twinge of sadness.

"You know, you have to be born again and again so you finally come to look just like him." Gentle judgment. I saw fire and a cross.

The preacher started to walk away. Blessed relief! I actually told him I had enjoyed talking to him. I lied. I just wanted him to go away. And then of course he turned around and came back. I strained to hear him again. He quoted something from Paul and assured me that *"brother"* meant *"sister"* too. At least my tormentor was sensitive to inclusive language!

He started to go again. He came back one more time and asked if I ever needed someone to do yard work. *"No."* He then asked if I had an old Bible he could take with him. *"I collect Bibles."* I noticed the outline of books through the side of his Adidas bag. *"No."* He smiled and said good-bye and walked away. Finally. Gentle judgment.

I experienced a rush of second thoughts. Of course I had an extra Bible. I remembered an unused one mailed to me by some society. I raced down the hall to my office and found the book. The preacher had never asked for money, though the implication was there that cash would come in handy. I pulled a few dollars from my billfold, tucked them into the Bible, and started up Peachtree Road in the direction he had gone. A strange sense of urgency was upon me. I also felt quite foolish and made sure the word "Bible" was not visible.

The preacher was nowhere in sight. Then I saw him across the street at Fellini's, a neighborhood pizzeria. He was talking to a group of shirtless young men sitting in the sun at the outdoor tables. No way was I going over there! I walked past, then turned around and walked back. But he had no intention of moving on up the street as I hoped. Instead, he went inside Fellini's, asked for a drink, came back out, and sat down at one of the tables. I was crushed, a proven wimp. So much for my convictions.

The preacher had spoken with power and authority; I, a representative of the institutional church, sitting on its very steps, had not. "I am the way." Before that afternoon I had found comfort and security in those words. "You can't get to God without dealing with me first," the preacher had said. Washed with the spray of his mouth, I now heard the warning, the challenge, the gentle judgment in those words. I saw a cross and spirit-fire.

The preacher was not just reminding me to tend to the old, the homeless, the wanderer---though he was not letting me off the hook, either. No, what I heard was even more compelling: he was calling us as the church to leave the safety of the stone steps---whatever they are for us--- and to walk across the street, to move out into the world and dare to speak with the authority conferred upon us in baptism. After all, we have been washed and sealed by the Spirit. We have been marked as Christ's own forever. We have been received into the household of God. We have been charged to confess the faith of Christ crucified, to proclaim his resurrection, and to share with all other saints in his eternal priesthood.

Later that afternoon I drove down Peachtree Road. No sight of him. The Bible remained on the back seat of the car for weeks after that, a reminder of the call of the preacher man.

Response and Restoration

*---- Will you proclaim by word and example
the Good News of God in Christ? ----*

ONE DAY RECENTLY I BECAME AWARE of a thudding
sound and discovered that a wren had flown inside the
house. The bird was repeatedly hurling itself against the
glass in an attempt to get out. I raced from room to
room, opening doors and windows as rapidly as I could,
and then tried to force it toward the nearest one with a
broom. Our movements grew increasingly frantic, and
the wren slammed hard into a wide pane and fell to the
floor. I picked it up and placed it outside on a ledge to
die. But there was another wren nearby. Singing wildly,
it flitted from branch to branch in the vicinity of that
ledge. The stunned bird blinked. It had heard the song!
Slowly it lifted its head, rose, staggered a few steps,
rested, and then swooped into the trees. A voice it
knew had called it back into life.

Within the biblical wisdom tradition there is the important insight that one way by which God reveals
truth, goodness, and beauty to us is through our careful
observations of the natural world and our imaginative reflections on these observations. The wren nearby, who
simply sang its song and in doing so made it possible for
the trapped wren to find its way to life, provided me

with an example of response and restoration. My reflections on this incident led me to consider the nature of the church's response to all that God has made if it is to be faithful to its vocation of restoration.

The mission of the church as stated in the prayer book is "to restore all people to unity with God and each other in Christ." This statement can be expanded to mean the redemption of the entire creation to that which God intends. It is a systemic statement: it says that we as church exist in order to be related to and share in the divine responsibility for all that God has made. While we are a distinct body and thus different from other bodies, we are inextricably connected to them and are to be involved with them. Only when we are in concert with our connectedness to all around us do we have the authority—the right—to exercise our power. Only then can we act on behalf of the reign of God.

We who call ourselves Christian are members of the church by virtue of our baptism, and we belong to the church for the duration of our lives. Our only decision, therefore, is how to live out or not to live out this belonging; we can do nothing about its reality. Our individual choices for action will be related to our own gifts and graces and to the particular opportunities for faithful response each of us is afforded because of circumstance or position. We can identify various faithful responses and then choose among them, using our own power and authority as God wills for us to do.

First, we can respond by going apart on behalf of others in order to pray constantly for them. This is the contribution of those who choose the extreme of the cloistered contemplative religious order. I think of a Discalced Carmelite sister. She lives by strict rules of diet, solitude, and silence in order to spend the major part of each day on her knees in a chapel in prayer, adoring God and interceding for the world. While I do not think I will ever join her number, I am grateful for her company among us and the reverberations of healing presence that flow from her community.

Second, we can withdraw and strive to form a perfect and uncontaminated community as a picture of what living into the reign of God is like. This is the contribution of a positive sectarian approach, such as the Amish communities in Pennsylvania. Their requirement of personal simplicity holds up a corrective mirror in which the self-serving and busy church can view itself. Their plainness in life and worship offers us alternative ways to consider. They can assist us in our pruning.

Third, we can strive to make the church itself a more exemplary and faithful community while continuing to live fully in our society, believing that simply by our presence there Christ will be represented and that our presence will make a difference. This is the choice of most faithful people, those who keep the wheels of the world turning—for better and for worse. It is the choice of those who move regularly between life in the world as teachers, students, doctors, nurses, patients, cooks, builders, managers, secretaries, parents, and friends, and life in the gathered company of Christ. It is the choice of those who daily struggle to connect the world and the altar, for the well-being of both.

For many, however, none of these responses will be enough, and they will choose a different one. Some of them will devote their primary energy to caring for the needy and neglected. They will identify with those who suffer the consequences of evil and will offer to the rest of us powerful examples of our own responsibility to care. I think of a bright young lawyer who gave up a promising practice to work with little girls and young women in a particularly bleak housing project. Through the power of her love, she is helping them forge a strong shield of self-esteem with which to ward off the demons of drug dependency and despair. She is pointing these girls into a future of promise for themselves. Through the power of her leadership, she brings others from her church with her to love and be loved as well.

Finally, there will be those who position themselves to engage in work for radical change in systems, those who exert pressure for political, economic, and environmental justice. Lobbying groups and community organizers are examples, as are those who provide food and shelter for our urban homeless while they press for the systemic change necessary to remedy the conditions contributing to the plight of those they serve. I think of a woman in my city who is a faithful member of her congregation and who heads a task force on homelessness. We frequently see her on the television screen during the hard months of winter as she publicly presses city and state officials to change immoral practices and laws. I know she also works hard behind the doors of board rooms and offices, and I have heard her privately describe personal fatigue and despair that is only alleviated by her regular participation in the worship and life of the company of Christ.

Followers of Jesus can choose how to take up their responsibility—their authority—to and for the communities to which they belong. They can adopt one or a combination of these responses, all of which are good and right and are mutually dependent on the others for the church's radical response to the needs of God's created order. These responses can shape and inform each other if taken together. A healthy church living in relationship to the whole of creation—God's company—will be about its mission to love the world that God loves so much.

Wings

— Do you promise to follow
and obey him as your Lord? —

THERE ARE THOSE TIMES ALONG THE WAY *when we are*
challenged by the promise and cost of being Christian,
times when we are to examine and rediscover our respon-
sibilities, seasons when we are to look at our lives as dis-
ciples of Jesus. In the ninth chapter of his gospel,
Matthew confronts us with a summary of Jesus' ministry
and thus of ours:

> Jesus went about all the cities and villages, teaching in
> their synagogues, proclaiming the good news of the
> kingdom, and curing every disease and every sickness.

So we are to move around, to be on our feet. We are
not a sit-on-our-duffs people. We are to be out and about,
teaching, proclaiming, and healing. None of these three is
isolated from the other two. We teach with our healing;
we heal with our teaching; we teach and heal with our
proclamation of the good news of God in Christ. And
that news is indeed good: "My reign is at hand! You no
longer have to be anxious and afraid. I, God, am in
charge. I love you even as you are. You are my people,
and if you stay with me you will soar on the wings of
eagles."

> When he saw the crowds, he had compassion for them,
> because they were harassed and helpless, like sheep
> without a shepherd.

The language here is strong and vivid. An English translation cannot do the meaning justice; in the Greek, "had compassion for" is the strongest expression for pity. It comes from the same root as the word "bowels." Jesus was moved to the very depth of his being. "Harassed" and "helpless" can be rendered "mangled, plundered" and "laid prostrate."

The scenes on which we look demand the same response. Scenes of the unremitting and crippling carnage in Africa and Latin America and Central Europe. Small children dying in drive-by shootings as they gaze through dirty windows in dreary housing projects. Haunting images of the gaunt faces of AIDS, increasingly before us in elevators and offices. Racial violence among the hopeless young on the streets of our cities. Pitiful snapshots of the blanketed homeless lying in dark and filthy doorways. Dirty rivers pouring over their molested banks, protesting our ongoing neglect of the created order.

If we are not dead in our core, we are moved to the very depths of our being. And what are we to do? We are to proclaim, to teach, and to heal. God's will for us and for the whole of creation is that we soar together on the wings of eagles.

Jesus says to his disciples----to those twelve and to us: "There is much to do. The harvest is vast, and I need many workers. I will give you all the authority you will need to be about my work of healing, proclamation, and teaching."

There are two things to notice about the twelve Matthew names for us. First, they are just ordinary people---- not especially learned, not particularly well-placed in society, not known for their public speaking. We might say that these founding leaders of our church were extraordinary only in that ordinariness. On any given day this realization can either relieve us or challenge us, but it does not let us off the hook.

The second thing we can note is that the twelve are an unlikely combination of souls: Matthew, who collected taxes for the Romans, and Simon, who probably had been a member of the Zealot party, those prepared to go to any measure to free themselves from the hated Roman rule. Parker Palmer has described the true church as that place where the people you like least belong, and as soon as one of them leaves, someone you like even less takes his place! And isn't that just what the body of Christ is supposed to be: an unlikely collection of women and men who might not choose each other in any other setting but who now are glued together by that work of teaching, proclamation, and healing----work carried out in response to the boundless grace which continuously washes over us?

Jesus gives his disciples instructions, rules for the road. There are two that seem particularly compelling for us today.

First, "Go nowhere among the Gentiles, and enter no town of the Samaritans, but go rather to the lost sheep of the house of Israel." This admonition reflects the prior call and peculiar responsibility of the Jews as God's own holy people, chosen by God to bring God's blessing and promise to the entire world. But it can remind us today that we cannot go everywhere. We cannot be all things to all people. It also implies that if we do not stand for something----if we have no identity----we have nothing to offer.

Jesus adds to the thrust of this admonition a bit later when he says, "If anyone will not welcome you or listen to your words, shake off the dust from your feet as soon as you leave that house or town." We have the authority---- the responsibility----to make decisions about when and where we teach, proclaim, and heal. We are not to batter our heads against brick walls. Taking up the cross of Christ and losing one's self for the sake of the gospel have never meant being blatantly stupid or disrespectful of one's own time and effort. So we must choose. We must focus our energies if we are to heal, teach, and proclaim faithfully. We cannot soar----even on the wings of eagles---- if we do not know our limits and our boundaries.

Jesus' second rule for us today: "Take no gold, or silver, or copper in your belts, no bag for your journey, or two tunics, or sandals, or a staff...." In other words, we are to travel light. The work of proclaiming, teaching, and healing requires our being free to move ahead with spirit and grace, open to miracle, open to the unimaginable. We are to resist colluding with the culture in its definitions of success and effectiveness. We are to step back from our love of accumulating and hoarding. We are to put down our heavy bags of grudge and grievance. We are to ask ourselves, "Of what are we to let go so we can go forth?" We cannot soar if we are weighted down by so much baggage.

I don't think anyone would deny the world's great need in the face of the cries bombarding us from all sides. Yet we will not be overwhelmed if we remember these two rules of Jesus' road: Know your limits, your boundaries; and travel light. But of course there is so much more to help us, and the symbols are all around:

We have a God who loves and treasures us, even at our worst.

We have a leader who has gone before into all we will encounter.

We are not impotent; we have been given the power and the authority to teach, to proclaim, and to heal in God's name.

We have each other for company and support.

We have the beauty of the whole creation to delight us and make us sing.

We have the bread and the wine for nourishment and strength.

Listen! Can you hear it----the whirring sound of wings? We can soar if we are willing to mount the backs of eagles!

Illumination

— Send them into the world in witness to your love. —

MOUNTAINS ARE PLACES TO WHICH WE GO *for a variety of reasons: for inspiration, for restoration and transformation, for the marshalling of resources to meet whatever lies ahead. Guided by an angel of the Lord, the prophet Elijah goes to the holy mountain of God to escape. After defeating and slaying the prophets of Baal, he is fleeing for his life from the wrath of Jezebel, wife of Ahab, apostate king of Israel.*

Alone and discouraged, Elijah lodges in a cave and wraps himself in misery. He is slumped in the meanness of his spirit when God passes by. There is great wind, earthquake, and fire; but God is not in these. Then after the fire comes a still small voice. The Hebrew is, "a sound of gentle stillness"----the deep quiet that vibrates with meaning and possibility, the quiet that speaks through our chatter and cries, the quiet that sings love songs to our souls.

Elijah stirs and moves to the entrance to the cave, wrapping his face in his mantle as he stands before the Holy One: the One from whom he hoped against hope to hear, the One he dreaded to face in his humiliation. God simply asks, "What are you doing here, Elijah?" The words contain both rebuke and comfort. "Why have you fled, Elijah? Didn't you know I would find you----always find you?" Elijah recites all that he has done in God's service----to no avail. And God responds: "Go, return.

There is work yet to be done, and there will be company for you in that work. Remember, I will not leave you alone." Strengthened, Elijah comes down.

On his path to the cross, Jesus takes Peter, James, and John and goes up on a high mountain. He goes to pray and to prepare for his ordeal. He goes to await God's word. On the mountain Jesus' appearance, his countenance, is transformed. His clothes become dazzling with unknown whiteness. Before us is the resurrected Christ. Before his death, we see his glory. We now know how the story will turn out. His and ours. The ending is told before the plot is unraveled in detail.

Granted, this is ordinarily a strange and disappointing way to tell a tale. How many of us have not sneaked a look at the last page of the book and regretted doing so? But when we are talking about the story that gives us courage and power to move into the uncertainty of our lives with confidence and resolution, the ending is a splendid gift indeed. We will not know the in-between events until they happen; we will not know the exact manner of our deaths in advance. But we do know that God will be with us in them all. God has liberated creation from all that death can hurl against life.

On the mountain the transfigured Jesus talks to Moses and Elijah, who represent the fullness of Jewish tradition----the law and the prophets----uniting Hebrew scripture with that which is to come. Luke tells us that the three speak of Jesus' "departure" which is about to be accomplished in Jerusalem. The transfiguration thus gives us the true meaning of Jesus' life: that Jesus is the glorious son of God and that messiahship and our discipleship involve suffering. In the transfiguration, we catch a glimpse of eternity----a glimpse of the profound change in the world to come, a glimpse of the fulfillment of God's promises. But there is that cross in the way.

Terrified, Peter stammers to Jesus, "Rabbi, it is good for us to be here; let us make three dwellings, one for you, one for Moses, and one for Elijah." He does not know what else to say. Perhaps Peter wants to prolong the glorious experience. More likely he is saying: "God forbid! Things cannot go in the way they seem to be heading. Maybe I can offer an alternative God will accept instead."

Even as Peter speaks, the holy cloud comes and overshadows them. Echoing the pronouncement at Jesus' baptism, the voice says: "This is my Son, the Beloved; listen to him! Listen to him! He has the words you must hear. Obey him." The voice is addressing the disciples and us. We are to hear what we often prefer to ignore, to welcome what we may not want to receive, to embrace what seems to make no sense, to live lives we might choose to change. God says to Peter and to the church, "Listen to Jesus."

Like Peter we resist accepting the cross as the means God chooses to realize the divine reign of peace and justice. It is not easy to believe that an ignominious death between two criminals is the way God chooses to conquer evil forever. It goes so against the grain, so against the success-driven culture in which we are immersed. Our coins may read "In God we trust," but if we appear to trust in God too much----rather than money, power, possessions, and the like----we are likely to be ridiculed or dismissed as irrational and irresponsible.

The transfiguration is a story about time and the problem of time. Like Peter, we can mistake the future for the present. Like Peter, we can want to make booths----to avoid or deny the way we are to travel, to avoid hovering on the future's threshold, to avoid dwelling in the fierce tension between the already and the not-yet. But we who abide in the bright side of Easter can believe in new possibility, in God's restoration of creation. We have seen the transfigured and resurrected Christ and so can choose to live lives of vulnerability that make no sense to the world. Our glimpse of God's future gives us the power to prevail as God's people of hope and peace, able to deny and transcend the deathly messages bombarding us daily.

When Jesus and the disciples come down from the mountain, they are met by a large crowd, as we too are met by demanding voices from which we cringe and long to turn away, those for which we have no time in our building of booths. A distraught man emerges, requesting healing for his only son, a boy possessed of a spirit that convulses and exhausts him. The other disciples have been unable to cast it out. The Jesus glorified on the mountain now must act on the plain, now must deal with a demon.

The story of Jesus' transfiguration and that of the boy's healing are to be considered together; they stand in absolute relationship. The exalted Jesus is disturbed by the suffering thrust upon him, and he is disappointed by the doubting impotence of his disciples. "You faithless generation, how much longer must I be among you? How much longer must I put up with you? Bring him to me." His stinging words indict us as well.

We need the vision of the transfiguration so we can go on, but we are to go on. We are not to build booths of security, of escape, even if they are monuments to moments of grace and transformation. Like Elijah, Peter, James, and John, we are to come off our mountain-top experiences----whatever they may be----and choose to return to the plain. We are to deal with demons. We are to move into our everyday lives and work bearing the good news of God in Christ, and the glorious God who reigns from the empty arms of the cross gives us the power to do so.

Third Movement

BAPTISM AND RESPONSIBILITY

Heavenly Father, we thank you that by water
and the Holy Spirit you have bestowed
upon these your servants the forgiveness of sin,
and have raised them to the new life of grace.
Sustain them, O Lord, in your Holy Spirit.
Give them an inquiring and discerning heart,
the courage to will and to persevere,
a spirit to know and to love you,
and the gift of joy and wonder in all your works.

Indispensable

---- Will you strive for justice and peace among all people, and respect the dignity of every human being? ----

THE OCCASION WAS AN ELDERHOSTEL RETREAT. It was entitled "Using Your Spiritual Gifts," and I was the weekend's inexperienced leader. On Friday evening I asked the group to draw their spiritual journeys in whatever ways they liked. I gave each person a large sheet of newsprint, a supply of colored magic markers, and held my breath.

As they scattered to do their work, Ethel, a spry birdlike woman of eighty-six, approached me, wringing her hands. She was distraught: "I cannot do this. I don't know how to do this." She pleaded for a reprieve. My anxiety rose. What could I do with Ethel? Was the weekend doomed before it began? And the words came: "Ethel, can you *talk* about your life with God?" She snapped her response, "Certainly! God is my friend."

"Then write about your friendship; put your words on the paper," I proposed. Over her reluctance, I sat her down at a table, gave her a sheet of newsprint and a stack of markers, and held my breath again. Using a variety of colors, Ethel wrote a radiant psalm ending with the words, "There is no end to God's promises!" This psalm of praise came from a woman who had grown up in extreme poverty. An orphan, she had been forced to leave school at an early age and earn her way by working as a maid in the homes of the rich or as a nurse who tended the very sick. Yet in the telling of her story, Ethel only saw herself as chosen and blessed by God: "God is my friend; God has always been there with me."

There was another woman, Ruth. She was seventy-six and moved regally even with the use of a walker. There was something about the way she held her head that was queenly and elegant; her trademark was a series of rich scarves she flung around her shoulders with great panache. Ruth described her life to us as a "wonderful walk with God," and she later told me about her late husband and the marvelous trips they had taken together to France and Greece and England. She had studied music, too, but said that it now no longer gave her the intense pleasure it once had. Ruth saw herself as living through a dark night of the soul, with no awareness of God's presence. She protested: "God has put me on the shelf. I have come here this weekend to see if I can find God again—or if God can find me!" It sounded like a dare.

Ruth wanted to talk after lunch on Saturday and warned me there would be tears. We sat in rocking chairs on the central deck of the conference center, ignoring the comings and goings around us. Ruth tore two sheets of paper from a notebook: "These are for you." She had written an extended psalm of lament in which she was lost and alone, separate, as if peering at life through a veil. "I still have so much I want to give but no way to do so. I think I could be helpful to younger women. I have volunteered in my parish, but no one has followed through. I wish I didn't have to volunteer; it would be so nice to be chosen." And the words came: "God chooses you," I said, "and *I* choose you." Her eyes brightened and filled with tears. We continued to talk for quite a long time—about our lives and our families—

about nothing, about everything. Then Ruth took my hands in hers and prayed. Strength flowed between us. She went to her room for a nap and slept soundly. We had to awaken her for the next session.

Isaiah the prophet declares, "Here is my servant, whom I uphold, my chosen, in whom my soul delights...." The beloved who is chosen. And who among us does not long to be chosen by someone, for something, to be selected as the one, to be named? I can remember the anxiety of grade-school playgrounds where I waited to be picked by those marvelously athletic team captains. I can remember auditioning for parts in plays and for the cheerleading squad, then waiting and waiting for my name to be called. I can remember the teenage agonies of listening for the telephone to ring.

But the longing to be chosen does not depart with the passing of childhood. No, that longing grows more deeply intense in the run of time, when opportunities for being chosen seem fewer and fewer. For it is in being chosen—by someone, for something—that we know we are important, worthy, that we matter. And who among us does not want to matter to someone, for something? When we are chosen—by someone, for something—we are no longer alone.

At Jesus' baptism the voice from that torn-apart heaven proclaims, "You are my Son, the Beloved; with you I am well pleased." It is with his baptism that Jesus' identity as the chosen one of God is declared: Jesus, the beloved one chosen to serve and to die and to rise. And it is in baptism that our identity is also revealed, as the beloved chosen of God. Perhaps it would not be too fanciful to say that every time one of us is baptized the heavens open—just a little—and that voice pronounces blessing: "With you I am well pleased. I always have been, and now you know it." And that dove-like spirit again descends and hovers.

In baptism we choose to be grafted into the community of faith as followers of Jesus. We choose to make promises about living in this community, and the community in turn makes promises to uphold and to help us. In baptism we join Ethel and Ruth and the entire company of God's beloved; knowing ourselves as God's chosen ones, we will never be alone again.

But we can't stop here. We are not chosen for special privilege and favor. We are not chosen to enjoy being together. If we stopped here angry thunder would roll from that parted heaven; the dove would freeze in flight. We are chosen *by God*, and we are chosen *for something*. Like Jesus, we are chosen to serve and to die, with the promise that we will rise—again and again—and we are chosen to let all others know that they are chosen, too. If we are to give this message of good news to the others with whom we live and work, we must know who they are and the nature of our relationship to them. This requires beginning with a look at the creation in which God has placed us together.

As we look around us, it does not take us long to realize that God's odd pleasure seems to have been to make no two things exactly alike: no two birds, no two leaves, no two anything. Rather than bland sameness, God seems to favor rich color and changing scene; woven tapestry and contrapuntal conversation, albeit accented by plain cloth and silence. We don't know why. At first blush God's plan does not seem practical or economical. If all were alike, there would not be as many variations, as many choices, as many decisions. One answer would suffice, for there would be only one question. It seems that uniformity would have been simpler for God—and for us—to manage. But maybe good management isn't what God is after. Or, more likely, we do not understand what it means.

We women and men are part of this creation of color and diversity; no one of us is like any other who has been, is now, or will be. No two athletes have the same moves, no two artists the same brushwork. No one has exactly the same skin shade as someone else—or the same thoughts. Each of us views the world through a different lens from a different angle. We are originals. This reality is both exhilarating and sobering, and it also has several consequences.

First, each of us is indispensable. Since no one else is exactly like you or me, no substitutions are possible. This thought is both humbling and fearsome. It is God who has made me unique, God who has deemed me different; I cannot take credit. Someone has defined humility as the patient pursuit of one's own excellence, meaning that faithfulness to God's design lies in striving to be all God intends us to be. The musical virtuoso is humble only as she claims and uses her genius to God's glory. If I and I alone can inhabit my piece of ground— wherever or whatever it is—then this place of holiness will be empty if I am not there.

Second, all others are indispensable as well. They are to dwell on their pieces of holy ground if the present creation is to be whole. Every life is of value and worth. We are dependent upon one another because each one of us sees truth from a different perspective, even if the difference is imperceptible. How presumptuous we are to think we have a corner on the market of the truth! Paradoxically, we are knit and bound together by our differences more than by our similarities. The orchestra can bring to life a symphonic score only as the various instruments with their distinctive tones and timbres are played together. If all of us were alike, we would need no one in the room but ourselves. How lonely and dull such existence would be—devoid of color and pattern, rhythm and rhyme.

Third, we are to call forth contrast and variance. We are to encourage the expression of differences, not their suppression. This is the work of the one who makes peace—the work of reconciliation, the work of the church. Peace is never achieved by the denial of discord. The hard work of the negotiator is to help us place our differences squarely on the conference table so that we can scrutinize and weigh them and compare them to each other. Only then do we have a chance of coming to graceful and creative solutions. To be who we are—creators in the image of the Creator—we are to be engaged in the setting free those whom we meet to be who they are: those different from us, those who will see and hear from other perspectives, those who will not agree with us or with each other. To aim for anything less is stifling and destructive—particularly for the ones named to be God's people of life.

Royal People

THE WRITER OF THE FIRST LETTER of Peter calls us a royal priesthood, the royal people of God. Perhaps we hear faint trumpets in the background heralding such a marvelous announcement with brilliant fanfare, and we graciously respond, "Yes, of course; thank you." After all, we are privileged persons by the standards of most of the world; we live in a privileged and powerful nation, a nation whose ways and future we know are blessed by God. We are even members of a church largely constituted of other privileged ones. And to those with active imaginations, the notion of royalty can conjure up images of majestic purple robes and horse-drawn carriages pulling up before turreted castles.

But more likely we shrink back in embarrassment at the audacity of the words. As we look around the room at each other, we know better. We are just ordinary people with our share of inadequacies and failures. This unknown writer cannot possibly be saying what is true for us, we who are so painfully conscious of the tattered rags that veil our hearts, the pile of sticks that betray the ruins of relationships. The shelves of our souls can seem bare indeed. Baggy sweaters and secondhand cars are what we deserve, not purple robes and carriages.

But wait. We have taken "royal priesthood" out of context, a silly practice at best. If we put it back, we can see ourselves as God intends us to be; we can bathe in the rich grace of the metaphor and be about the work to which God is ever calling us. You see, the writer of 1 Peter also calls us a holy people, God's own people, chosen to witness to the rays of hope and freedom emanating from the risen one. The root word from which "royal" is derived is the Latin regere, to rule, to lead. As God's people we are to lead others from the darkness of despair and bondage, whatever form that bondage takes. We are to be rulers in God's present and coming reign. But this reign is different from the monarchies of the world. It is a reign that begins with a cross. It is a reign of service. It is a reign in which the last are first and first are last.

I want to tell you the true story of a gift I received several winters ago. The setting is a men's shelter in Atlanta that provides food and temporary lodging. I serve as a volunteer there for the purpose of cleansing my soul. In the middle hours of one night, I encountered a man named Christopher in the lighted hall between the room housing a laboring washing machine----its tub futilely churning load after load of dirty, dark water----and the darkened sleeping room with its lines of disinfected cots. The blue plastic mattresses cradled bodies of men with nothing left to do but wrap up in thin blankets and lie down with whatever the night would bring or deny.

Christopher was short in stature, with missing teeth and a protruding belly. He talked on and on about his life; I mostly listened, nodding when some response seemed expected. He was a brick layer from the mountains of Tennessee, and had come to Atlanta to find work. He wistfully described the winding dirt roads over which he had walked as a child. He told about his marriage at nineteen to a woman of thirty-eight who was already five or six months pregnant. He told of a white collie he had found, fed, washed, and named King. The dog was stolen by a preacher and resold. Christopher admitted his capacity for violence, relishing his desire to "smash" those he judged responsible for his lot in life, particularly his father.

After a while I began wondering how to free myself from the chilling flow of his words. But then he said, "God has blessed me; God has let me see the darkness so I would know the light." And I thought of Isaiah's words about those who walked in darkness.

He inquired, "Do you have a Bible?" "Yes," I responded. "Do you have it with you?" "No, it's at home." He continued, "I want to give you something." And he disappeared into the shadows of the sleeping room. I waited.

He emerged with a tattered, white New Testament in his hands. He opened it and produced a perfect specimen of a monarch butterfly. "I want you to have this. I found it on a road in Tennessee. I have kept it in here for a long time." I protested. He insisted. I put out my hand and accepted the butterfly from his. "Will you promise to put it in your Bible, the one you use?" he asked. I gave my pledge and mumbled my thanks. Christopher withdrew into the territory of the blue cots.

The butterfly is in a white envelope, always somewhere among the pages of my well-worn Oxford Annotated. It continues to surprise me when it flutters forth.

A woman like me is on shaky ground when she tells a story from the domain of the homeless. But she is on even shakier ground if she does not recognize those who mysteriously bear the image of Christ and if she does not accept the tokens of new life they offer. After all, those who heard the angels' announcement of divine birth were shepherds, humble and untrustworthy. The God who entered human life and who died there is frequently known best by those with the greatest need and the least to lose.

We do well to heed their testimony, for they remind us that:

> *We are to travel light, willing to live lives of downward mobility in an upwardly-driven world.*
>
> *We are to be involved in the stuff of that world, with dirty hands and stained clothes.*
>
> *We are to identify with those who suffer, for we too know the pain of disappointment and loss.*
>
> *We are to protect those who are vulnerable, for we join them in feeling exposed and unprotected.*
>
> *We are to eat with those who are hungry, for we too long for the nourishment that sustains our spirits.*
>
> *We are to sleep with those who are without bed and home, for we are also travelers through the dark night.*
>
> *We are to lay down our lives.*

At baptism we are grafted into a royal household, the company of Christ; the body for which Christ is the living cornerstone, the foundation; the community meant for worship, witness, and loving service. It means that we never have to rely on our own self-sufficiency because our certainty comes from beyond ourselves. Our lives, our vocations, our holy dignity find their origin in the central, unshakable pattern of God's redemptive will for the entire creation. We are God's royal people.

Children of Wrath

— Deliver them, O Lord, from the way of sin and death. —

SEVERAL SPRINGS AGO I WAS WALKING *down a street in Salzburg with a small group of colleagues on a rainy Sunday afternoon. We had eaten lunch together, a meal during which I had begun to feel more and more miserable and isolated; more and more locked inside my own shell. One difficulty was that of language----I speak no German. My sense of isolation was increased by the fact that I was the only woman there and the only person who was not a priest. So there we were, walking down that street in the rain, with me in angry and self-absorbed silence.*

Suddenly Tony, one of the Roman Catholic priests in our group, broke from our ranks and headed for several beggars huddled against a building. He gave them a few coins and engaged them in a moment of conversation. Then to my horror, Tony and one of the men headed straight for us----straight for me! Tony was smiling and waving an arm reassuringly. "Wait; it's all right. Don't be afraid; he just wants to shake your hand." I stopped. The man approached eagerly, offering a toothless smile, hand extended. I smiled in return and held out mine to him. Two people with nothing in common but their humanity greeted each other and touched.

The beggar ducked his head and then dropped down on one knee in a courtly bow. Still holding fast to my hand, he kissed it quickly but tenderly. He rose. I stammered my thanks----"Danke schön." We looked each other in the eye for a number of seconds before breaking our clasp. Then he mumbled a few sentences in rapid German and began weeping softly. Tony intervened again: "It's all right. He is saying that he misses his family. You remind him." Tony comforted the man, and we walked away.

At the risk of romanticizing, I call this event an encounter of grace. Certainly the situation was complex, and I cannot say what went on for Tony or for the beggar man. For me, I was reengaged, my isolation broken. The gentle beggar saw. He did not avert his eyes. He acknowledged me. He honored me. His actions----albeit unaware----invited me back into community. I experienced reconciliation with myself and with the others. I experienced the Christ in the words and gesture of this man I met that day along the way of the journey.

We are not saying anything new when we liken the Christian life to a journey, a journey of ever living into our baptism. But if we are wise we remind ourselves that this journey of life is one which begins in death. In his letter to the Ephesians Paul describes the walk in death: "All of us once lived among them in the passions of our flesh, following the desires of flesh and senses, and we were by nature children of wrath, like everyone else." If we are honest in looking back over the experiences of our lives, we will not dismiss his words too quickly.

While we are not to disregard those moments when God's light breaks in around us along our journey, we are all too aware of ruts and rocks in the road. We are all too aware of our failures in relationships----the times we could not give to our spouse, friend, parent, or child. We are all too aware of good deeds done in the commu-

nity or at the office in self-interest, out of duty or to earn love and respect; the visits to shut-ins made in the hope of standing before God as "good" women and men. We have fooled no one.

This deathly road is a lonely one, for we finally are cut off----alienated from God and from each other. But the paradox of the gospel is that when we come up against the solid wall of hopelessness rising before us, around which we can see no path and over which there is no way; when we acknowledge ourselves as the sinners we are; then we are open to receive the gifts of God's love, forgiveness, and mercy. God's wrath is not the opposite of divine love; God's wrath is the result of divine caring. The wall----itself a gift of God----crumbles in the hand of God, and the path of hope opens before us. We come alive. We are free to leave the past behind and to move ahead into the richness God has intended all along.

Released from the past, we stand in the now, able to make our way into the future. The path will still be unknown. There will be ruts and rocks and walls through and around which there may seem to be no way. But we now walk in the presence and power of the Holy One and in the company of God's people, the church----the community of those reborn into relationship with God and with each other. It is our holy home, a foretaste of what is to come.

Creativity and Conflict

---- Through [water] you led the children of Israel out of their bondage in Egypt into the land of promise. ----

A TEACHER OF MINE ONCE SAID: "It is my job to be as right as I can be; it is your job to prove me wrong when you can. If we both do our work well, we will be about the task of education. But if you accept everything I say without challenge, you will render me ineffective as a teacher and will destroy our purpose." He was inviting his students to join a mutual quest for what is and for what can be. Although he was appealing for us to enter into struggle with him and with each other, I never sensed he was setting up adversarial or combatant relationships. Rather, he was describing the struggle inherent in creativity; the struggle of connecting interlocking puzzle pieces, of sliding them this way and that until the proper fit is found.

We are created to be unique, to be originals. We also are created to live in community; we are given the gift of each other. God creates the man, but God also sees that it is not good for him to be alone, and God makes the woman—symbol of all companions—different from the man *and* fit company for him. We are created separately—the molds are broken—*and* we are created to complement and complete each other—bones from our bones, flesh from our flesh.

When we can see ourselves as connected to each other and to the whole of creation, we can be freed from the terrible burden of forever being right. We can admit the failures we know all too well. Our questions can become: "What do you perceive that I have not seen? How is my understanding partial or erroneous?" *Together* we can set aside our dangerous delusion of independence and separateness. We can come closer to telling God's truth. We can participate in God's creative designs.

The creative process, even when for a time we are working alone, invariably involves tension and conflict. Any of us who have written a letter or a poem, who have painted a picture or a wall, who have raised roses or puppies or children can attest to that! There are periods of anxiety—bordering on terror—when the muse abandons, hope evades, and the sheet of paper or the canvas or the computer screen remains blank. There are stretches of swirling chaos when multiple images blur and order is elusive. There can even be times of temporary resolution before the swirl begins to whirl once more.

A bit dramatic? Perhaps. But conflict—understood as seeking and welcoming freshness and newness—is part of the divine plan. It is God's gift to us:

> Do not remember the former things, or consider the things of old. I am about to do a new thing; now it springs forth, do you not perceive it?

The conflict of disruption and discontinuity is not merely inevitable, as we tend to assume; instead, it is integral to God's order.

The word "conflict" is derived from the Latin *confligere*, to strike together—to make spirited sparks of passion and life. Conflict does not merely provide us with energy, insight, and possibility as by-products. Rather, newness comes only *with* conflict. The conflicted state is not a condition to be endured; instead, it is one to be sought and cultivated. Labor and birth are not for the faint of heart, however, and we do not usually employ such words in describing our approach to conflict. We talk about avoiding and managing.

The root of "manage" is the Latin *manus*—hand—and when I think of hands, I go back again to the ancient story of creation, this time envisioning Michelangelo's *The Creation of Adam* from the ceiling of the Sistine Chapel. Here God's hand reaches toward Adam's, forefinger extended. In my imagination a spark sizzles in the space between them as God sets it all in motion. God says: "Be different, Adam. But you will not be alone in your differentness. There will be other different ones. Create with them." God's hand is open, though tensed. God is not picking up Adam and shaking him into life, but inviting him to be. God is not touching Adam, but giving him room to respond and to experience his own vitality.

Michelangelo's genius provides us with fresh perspective on the meaning of management. Hands can be instruments either for checking, holding back, taking, restraining, and strangling or for guiding, pointing, stroking, kneading, giving away, and letting go. The issue is one of control.

As we accept God's gift of freedom from our sinful obsession with being in control, we recognize that management of people, of institutions, and of conflict has more to do with allowing than with suppressing. We become able to open doors and windows to bracing winds of difference and diversity, no longer condemned to slamming them shut in the face of anyone or anything bearing threats of change—or even of truth. In this light, violence and war are not conflict run amuck, conflict out of all bounds, but the outcomes of conflict quelled. They result when we will not allow difference, when we deny our life-giving dependence on others—those different ones—with all our might and means.

A question emerges: If conflict is the given of creation and the creative process, why do we resist it so and why are we so fearful? Why are we threatened by any who dare to ask questions about the way things are, who dare to offer challenges about the way things could be—perhaps are meant to be? Why do we seek to evade those who want something to be different: blacks, gays, women, the elderly, children, the poor, the sick? The list may change over time, but it still goes on and on.

We are fearful because conflict is the forerunner of birth. We cling to the comfortable and predictable because they are comfortable and predictable, and we think we can control them. Remember the story of the people of Israel. Continuation of slavery became preferable to the unknowns of wilderness hope: "If only we had meat to eat! We remember the fish we used to eat in Egypt for nothing, the cucumbers, the melons, the leeks, the onions, and the garlic; but now our strength is dried up, and there is nothing at all but this manna to look at." We can stay in damaging relationships and continue deathly habits because any other alternative is too terrifying to imagine. With those ancient wilderness wanderers, we can long to remain in our bondage—whatever it may be—because that prison is known and manageable, in our perverted and sinful sense of the word.

And sadly, we resist conflict because it is the result of the differences between us. We have not been helped to prize our uniqueness, so we don't like it, believing that if we are different, we are not beautiful. The young dancer from *A Chorus Line* says it well: "Now different is nice, but it sure isn't pretty; pretty is what it's about. I never met anyone who was different who couldn't figure that out." The skinny little girl with brains hides her way with words under the guise of shyness, dreading the ostracism she knows will occur if anyone learns the awful truth about her. The playful but unathletic little boy manages a wheezing attack the morning of every grammar school field day in his attempt to remain under cover.

Not only do we dislike our own distinctness, we do not appreciate the peculiarity of God's other beautiful children. Phrases like "We have so much in common" or "We are so much alike" roll off our tongues, while "We are so different" sticks in our throats. In our insecurity we are afraid of these strangers. We do not trust our ability to stand with them; we do not recognize the divine spark between us. The consequence of this fear and distrust is that we can find ourselves alienated and isolated, denied the richness of connection and relationship. Painter and engineer hold each other at arm's length, failing to see in the other's unique offering something they cannot provide on their own—on the one hand a world of shapely color, on the other a comfortable and easy environment in which creativity can flourish.

Conflict—managing our differences—throws the paradox of our creation into high relief: we are single, yet united; solitary, yet communal. The issue is one of survival. If we dare enter the wilderness into which our differences propel us, we fear we will lose our identities or our relationships, or both. We will be merged into the image of another—no longer ourselves—or we will find ourselves alone, or both.

Resistance to conflict is our attempt to control and to manage in our own way, to eat the forbidden fruit of the tree. It is our effort to hide behind flimsy coverings of leaves, not daring to stand before God and each other in vulnerability that is strength. Our resistance to conflict—the appropriate and healthy managing of differences—is sin. As its consequence, we find ourselves expelled from the garden of relationship and cast into an arid exile of isolation, wandering, and death.

Yet courage has been defined as fear saying its prayers. So our only way out is to name our predicament what it is—sin—and to fall on our knees, to confess and to ask forgiveness. We are to hear that our fearful resistance and our prideful need to control have been overcome. What we cannot do under our own power has been made possible by the power of God's grace. As we begin the journey back into community, we soon recognize the ground beneath our feet. It is neither foreign nor untested. We have walked here before, and we have heard the stories of others who have been here. We recall our own stories, those past times when we were filled with the spirit of discovery and saw something emerge we did not necessarily expect or order— but *something*.

Sinner

STOLEN! MY HANDBAG HAD DISAPPEARED *from the bottom drawer of my desk. There was more money in it than I usually carry; I was about to leave on a week's trip. There were the expected driver's license, credit cards, and banking card. There was also a pair of gold earrings, a treasured gift from old friends. There were the keys to my apartment, office doors, and my new car. I was flooded with feelings of disbelief, disorientation, and self-doubt. I felt as if I were to blame.*

Colleagues rallied around. One drove me to the house of a friend who had a key to my apartment while another found cash for my trip. The car was so new that templates were not available and a locksmith could not make duplicate keys, so a tow truck moved it to my apartment until I could figure out what to do. Someone else provided a ride to the airport. I was uncomfortable in needing so much help. Who likes to be that dependent?

A shopping center security guard found my bag a week later in an alley. Cash and earrings were gone. So were my keys. The recovery didn't seem to matter much, and finally neither did the losses. The damage lay in that sense of personal violation and in the ensuing inconvenience. I made reports to the police and my insurance company. I canceled my cards and changed the locks on the doors to my apartment. There had been other thefts, so my employer changed the office locks. The car remained vulnerable. I threw away the wallet, now a contaminated thing.

I grieved, but mostly I remained angry and suspicious. My colleagues and I watched for unfamiliar activity. We fingered likely suspects (we were sure it was an inside job!). One day we even planted a bag and watched for a repeated attempt, but to no avail. How dare the thief intrude upon my life when I needed it least? He (we were sure it was a man!) probably took the money to support a drug habit. Why didn't he just take the cash? Why did he have to mess with my things? I hoped he would be caught and given what he deserved. How I would have liked to get my hands on him!

That is how I felt and what I wanted to do. I am a good and responsible person, and I was indignant in that goodness. To make matters worse, the bag was stolen from within the walls of the church----of a cathedral no less. The locks were church locks. The colleagues inconvenienced included a bishop and a priest. Shouldn't we in the church be immune from this kind of thing? Shouldn't those who pass through our doors and who work for us be grateful to us? Shouldn't they be aware of who we are and for what we stand? No one should steal in a church.

With passing days the shock faded. I tired of telling the story to anyone who would listen. Nevertheless, I became increasingly aware of a creeping discomfort within me, and to my surprise I realized I was thinking about the thief instead of the theft. I wondered if he----or perhaps it was a she?----was someone I saw every day. I wondered what this person was contending with. I allowed myself to imagine desperation so deep that one might jeopardize a job for some measure of relief. I thought of the friends who had given me assistance. I wondered if this woman or man had anyone to offer some measure of mercy.

And then the revelation. For the first time I heard Jesus' words to the Pharisees: "Go and learn what this means, 'I desire mercy, and not sacrifice.' For I have come to call not the righteous but sinners."

Once again Jesus confronts and disturbs us. Jesus sees the image of God in the corrupt tax collector, Matthew. He invites sinners to his supper table. He says, "Eat with me now, as we will eat together in the reign of God." And the good news is that he sees the image of God in us as well, and he invites us to his banquet, too.

Still, we the baptized cannot eat with him until we are willing to recognize ourselves as sinners, as those who make sacrifices and offerings but do not love as he loves. Those who are righteously unmerciful. We will not hear the invitation to his meal until we concede the wrenching reality of our estrangement from God and then do the turnaround of repentance.

When we do, we find that the absence of God reverberates with God's presence. The God who faces away from our easy goodness finally does not permit us that ease. I think again of the person who took the bag. And now I think also of our connection. Will we see each other at the table to which we both are invited?

Confrontation

— Do you renounce the evil powers of this world which corrupt and destroy the creatures of God? —

AT ONE TIME MY FAMILY LIVED IN A HOUSE *buried deep in Atlanta's woods. My sons grew up playing adventure games among oak, pine, and hickory friends, building tree houses high in their leafy arms. My cats and dogs prowled in these woods, playing their own adventure games, as birds and squirrels shouted insults from the safety high above. These woods also afforded us certain and deep privacy; we had no need for blinds or curtains at the windows of our house.*

Then one spring everything changed. Bulldozers arrived. A road was cut into the woods. Every one of the large old trees was felled over a period of just a few days. The earth shook in protest every time one of them hit the ground. The sound was sickening and then numbing. My family and I were stricken and stunned. Granted, we would have liked nothing built back in there, ever, and I can admit that freely. But what happened was far beyond the invasion of twenty years of sylvan solitude. Nine large and expensive houses were eventually crammed into a space suitable for three at best. This was an obscenity, an instance of the trauma we can inflict in the name of progress.

One evening I saw the contractor walking amidst the devastation, and I impulsively headed out to confront him. I don't know when I have experienced such white-

hot rage. But even at the time my rage felt different from other occasions when I have been angry; even at the time I sensed this rage was "clean."

I spoke forcefully to the man. I used strong language. I accused him of rape. When he could find his tongue, he retaliated, "But this property isn't yours; it does not even belong to you." I countered, "It's not yours, either!" "You're talking religion to me, aren't you?" he asked. Taken aback, I allowed, "Yes, I guess I am." After a final verbal sally, I stalked back into the house. I was shaking, and I suspected he was, too. Still trembling, I later left for church. It happened to be Maundy Thursday, and I participated in the washing of feet.

I have thought about the incident many times in the ensuing years, and I never have experienced much guilt about what I said or did. The episode has remained clean for me, and over time it has come to remind me of a white-hot Jesus purging the temple, driving out those who are selling doves, overturning the tables of those who are changing money. In John's gospel we are told that he brandished a braided whip of cords. Jesus is challenging any notion that we can buy our way to God with our frantic rites and our church activity. He is judging our bustlings-about in the name of righteousness, saying that God is not interested in our sacrifices alone but in the goodness of our lives, in the ways we treat each other—particularly in his name.

Jesus does not seem to be set against the sale of animals for sacrifice or the changing of money for the payment of the required temple tax. Both are convenient for the worshiping Jew, particularly for those pilgrims traveling far distances to the temple. What Jesus protests is the shabby profiteering that served to swell the temple coffers, the greedy collusion between priest and trader carried out in the name of religion, sullying and staining the *worship of God. Our injustice to each other offends and dishonors the One in whose image we are made.*

God grieves when we relegate children of the present and the future to sterile land and gray pavement by our rapacious stripping and buildings, when we deny them the dance of water and the mystery of forest. Still, God invites us to join the process of creation. God gives us the freedom to be creators, but as our creations are wrenched away from God's purpose, they become tragically torn and disfigured. And then God holds us accountable. Our tables of pride ultimately are overturned, for the creation finally does not belong to us.

The contractor was right: the woods were not mine. I could not lock others out from building and living there, from enjoying them with me. But the woods were not his or mine to exploit, as though their existence meant nothing. We do not have the right to do anything we want to do.

Jesus lived within the historical context of his own time----as do we. He understood the need for institutional and worldly authority for order. He said to render to Caesar that which is Caesar's. But Jesus also was aware of the higher authority to which his allegiance, his responsibility, came first. And when these two authorities crossed with other, he named the conflict for what it was----with passion and with power----the power with which he starts a riot in the temple, the power with which he chooses to die on a cross. In both acts he confronts evil and names it. "Things are not to be as they are," he says. "This is not what God intends. You will see."

Where are we called to be prophets, the ones who say, "Things are not as they appear to be"? Everywhere. The temple is the scene of this story about Jesus, but as God's holy place it is the symbol of God's other holy places. Holy ground is anywhere we encounter God----and there is no place where God is not. The altar is the symbol of the street, the woods, and the marketplace. The place where we break and eat holy bread points to all other places where we break and eat bread—bread that also is holy. We are to declare "This is not what God intends" anywhere we see God's purpose thwarted and distorted.

But how do we know what God intends? An answer is found in the remainder of Matthew's version of the temple story. The blind and the lame come to him, and he heals them. "Hosannah to the son of David," the children in the temple sing out to him. God's purpose always brings healing and song. That is how we can recognize it.

The chief priests and the scribes were outraged by Jesus' acts that day, just as the powers around us will be disturbed by our acts of confrontation and expressions of divine freedom, but change never comes without disturbance and disruption. Jesus leaves and goes out of the city to Bethany to spend the night. It is enough for now; it is time to rest. He will return.

I am sure the buyers and the sellers moved right back into the temple, business as usual. Nothing changed—except that Jesus moved a stride closer to his death. Nothing changed—except that a few who had limped now walked tall and straight, and a few who had lived in darkness could see; a few silent children were singing now. Nothing changed in my neighborhood either. The nine houses were built. There is an ugly scar across the earth, a rip in the world. Perhaps another time the contractor will cut down fewer trees, build fewer buildings. But who knows?

Then one night I noticed the stars. I could see heaven through the gap where the trees once stood, and a message was there for me: After our work is done, after the bulldozers come, after we do all we can do—for worse and for better—God's grace, symbolized by those stars, will *still shine through. Jesus promised, "Destroy this temple, and in three days I will raise it up." We cannot ultimately destroy God's grace—our sin reveals grace all the more clearly. The question is not whether God's redemptive work will go on. It always has; it does; it will. The question is whether or not we will join in that work. Will we grasp the stars?*

Guidance
and Turbulence

---- Bring them to the fullness of your peace and glory. ----

THE CHURCH IS THE PLACE where we are equipped "to carry on Christ's work of reconciliation in the world." Part of this equipping must include our learning to confront each other so that we can confront the world with God's love. If we who claim to be created in the divine image and fed with the power of Christ's body and blood cannot entertain healthy conflict among ourselves, how can we expect to do so anywhere else?

Years ago someone gave me a new awareness of confrontation that has become one of my guiding precepts as I work in the church community and in the larger community of the creation. Confrontation means inviting others to join in because what we do matters, doing it together matters, and we are strong enough to withstand the sparks of disagreement. Invitation, engagement, consequence, relationship, respect—these are the hallmarks of confrontation as understood and practiced by the disciple of Jesus, not violation, force, intimidation, coercion, or disdain.

The word "confrontation" is derived from the Latin *com-frons* and means "placing foreheads together." While I suppose one could picture a painful butting of heads, my mentor's definition suggested instead the metaphor of the dance. In this light, I began to see our management of conflict as our moving together in time with the music because going our separate ways just does not work: we cannot be about the work of reconciliation God has entrusted to us as long as we remain apart. Over time I have developed eight guidelines that can help to direct us in our work. They apply to each of us personally and to the communities to which we belong.

1. Time. The question with which I too frequently begin a meeting is, "How long will this last?" rather than, "Have we allowed enough time?" Yet we are to grant gracious hours to the arduous but satisfying work of the creative process. The dance must not be rushed lest we lose contact with each other or stumble and fall. Being in each other's presence long enough to discover and appreciate our differences takes time; so does staying on as we sort through layers of disagreement.

Discovering legitimate common ground cannot happen in a hurry; receptivity to newness and change cannot be forced. Continuing and persevering and repenting and returning and proclaiming and seeking and serving and striving and respecting are the lifework of the baptized person. Trust takes time. Love takes time. Learning to dance takes time. Premature definitions of problem and solution are too often our heresy, inflexible schedules our curse. Welcoming complexity is ever the challenge.

2. Rhythm. Someone asks me, "Does seeking and welcoming our differences mean we will always be wrestling with each other? I am exhausted just thinking about it!" The writer of Ecclesiastes answers, "For everything there is a season, and a time for every matter under heaven." The creative process includes resolution and respite. God took the seventh day to rest, not as a time out but as an integral part of creating.

Further, our individual tolerances are not the same; we may want to whirl around the floor, barely move at all, or sit one out. We may prefer the waltz, the tango, or the jitterbug. "Speed up"; "Slow down"; "It's time to stop"; It's time to play"; "It's time to rest"; "I will decide"; "Please decide for us"—any of these can be a fitting response to personal and community needs in a particular moment.

3. Clarity. I have a friend who ends each gathering in his parish with a single question of evaluation: "How did our work contribute to God's reign of justice and peace?" He might go on, "Would Jesus have stayed for the whole meeting?" Creative work involves tension and conflict, and unless we have a clear idea of what we will be doing and why, we have no sane reason for setting ourselves up for increased stress.

All too often clarity is bypassed for a sloppiness we call expediency. We miss connecting with each other because we do not define the character of the dance. How many times I have come to realize in a particularly frustrating situation that we had wasted that time because we had not taken time to identify what matters to us and to state our purpose. I suspect that on occasion there is a more perverse reason for our neglect: if we are clear about what we are doing, something might happen! Further, what we say we intend to do and what we actually do are not always congruous, for the same kind of reason. Sharing in Christ's eternal priesthood can be costly—*there is that cross in the way.*

4. Structure. Suppose we had to guess what time a meeting was going to start and where it was going to be held every time a particular group gathered? I daresay that most of our available energy would be spent before we even began the task at hand. I also have been involved in conferences where a predetermined outcome was guaranteed by the excessive use of parliamentary procedure—no room for creative surprise here! We need enough structure to provide a dependable and consistent environment for taking risks; however, rigidity and inflexibility get in our way and stifle our search for freshness and change.

Providing structure means we are to be concerned with surroundings of space, time, and form, which are conditions necessary for unsettling work. Forums for the expression of differing opinions provide structure; so do agendas and clear avenues for asking questions and receiving answers. Our framework is to allow, guide, and shape, not to bind, confine, cut off, or control. When both partners are provided with the pattern of the steps of the dance, they are free to improvise.

5. Perspective. An executive of a major soft drink company told me, chuckling, "When things get too tense around here, we remind ourselves that our product—as fine as we believe it to be—is nothing but colored water with the right combination of sugar and flavorings." Rabbi Edwin Friedman warns of "reptilian regression," our going back to the state dictated by the reptile brain, a condition devoid of humor and the ability to laugh. It's not a very pretty picture.

Our pompous assumption that the forward roll of the universe rests on our own shoulders—a funny image if we think about it—only reveals our spiritual poverty. Keeping things in perspective means that we are not to take ourselves too seriously. Paradoxically, because *God* takes us seriously we can stand more easily and then can play, released to join the other dancers of creation.

6. *Storytelling.* We are to have places for the telling and hearing of stories and for the weaving of visions. I think of an animated dinner table conversation—voices rising and falling, hands moving, fingers pointing, ideas flowing. A primary place for us as people of God is the church, where around the eucharistic table we tell and hear the story upon which we bet our lives. It is a story of difference and conflict; a story of birth, death, and resurrection.

Power is released when persons and groups explore their unique stories—not just for the incredible joy of storytelling but because their stories gives them valuable clues about their heritage and their future. More than one person and community have found the courage to move into difficult times when they recollect that they have known the wilderness before and can witness to the promise on the other side. We also do well to remember that dance was the medium of our stories long before we could write the words.

7. *Guides.* Our guides are our beacons along the way of the dark night and our companions when the sun is bright and our steps are clear. They are our partners in the dance. We find guides in our communities. We meet them in the stranger on the road. We are to be open to their appearing in the unlikeliest times and places. I think of my encounters with the good Methodist ladies, the street preacher, and the sea. I think of children at liturgies, their high-pitched voices throwing new light on our entrance into holy mystery.

We who find ourselves in the role of guide are to be diligent lest we lose our own ways. Guides proclaim good news; they respect the dignity of every human being; they call us into repentance. Guides break bread and serve the Christ in all persons, extending God's hand of invitation. They pass on the spark of creation but do not get in the way. Each of us is both guide and guided; each of us is both Adam's descendant and God's sacrament.

8. *Prayer.* Prayer is being before God in expectation. Sometimes we are to be alone and quiet—in solitude and silence. Sometimes we are to be in the company of other praying souls—the company of Christ. Prayer is our time for conversation with God, and it is to be spent mostly in listening. God knows our thoughts before we speak them, while we have at best only glimmers of what God wants us to hear.

And because variation is the way of God's order, each of us will hear somewhat different words. We will find ourselves summoned to bring these differences back into the conversation of the community, to struggle once more in discovery of what God intends us to be and do—to work out the steps of the dance. But when we sit before God in expectation, we also become aware of the spirit that binds us together, that makes our living together in creative conflict possible. The Spirit is the source of God's windy grace ever blowing us into new life. We do well to remember the wisdom of the balloonist: without turbulence there can be no movement.

Heresy

— Give them an inquiring and discerning heart,
the courage to will and to persevere. —

MY EYE WAS CAUGHT AND HELD *by an interesting group
of sculptures in a small public exhibition space on New
York's Fifth Avenue. I went inside to pass some time
among them and chanced to meet the artist herself, Therese Censor, a diminutive Belgian Jew. Her slight build
and quiet, measured manner seemed at odds with the
power and passion revealed in her work. I soaked in the
spirit offered me by those figures of metal and stone and
slipped back out onto the sidewalk. It had been a pleas-
ant and satisfying interlude.*

*But that was not the end of it. One of the pieces stayed
with me, haunted me, in the days and weeks that followed. I was possessed by the thing. It was a small bronze
casting composed of three figures----a man, a woman, and
a child----leaning into each other. The piece was entitled,
"Blowin' in the Wind," and the old Bob Dylan song of the
sixties kept blowing around within me: "The answer, my
friend, is blowin' in the wind; the answer is blowin' in
the wind."*

*Its cost was beyond what I sensibly could afford, but I
made a gambler's deal with myself anyway. I was sched-
uled to return to New York in a couple of weeks, and if
the sculpture was still unsold, I would buy it. It was, and
I did.*

Therese gave me careful instructions regarding its placement on the rough, slate base. "They are going uphill against the wind," she stressed. She had caught the essence of a swirling, whirling wind, one that both held the figures back and pushed them along at the same time.

Silence followed, and then Therese asked, "Do you know what it is like to struggle uphill against the wind?" She posed the question to me straight on. Her artist's eyes pierced me to the quick, and I knew that my ownership of the sculpture----if one ever owns a piece of art!----swayed with my answer.

"Yes, I do know."

She believed me. We shook hands and promised to keep in touch. I carried "Blowin' in the Wind" in a canvas tote bag emblazoned with the words "Amazing Grace" back through Manhattan streets and on a plane to Atlanta.

Job was a man who could have thrown Therese's straight-on question right back at her: "You bet I know what it's like to struggle uphill against the wind! You bet I do!"

The book of Job is the story of an impatient, defiant, and familiar man. Stunned by first the loss of his wealth, then of his sons and daughters, and finally of his health, Job is buttressed only by his day's rigid theology of reward and punishment, pounded home to him in turn by three friends: "You have done something to deserve all this. Confess it, and your present misery will end."

But Job isn't buying their charges. Sin? Sure. But ordinary everyday stuff, nothing to bring on all of this! And he begins cursing the day of his birth, hurling violent protest after protest to God, his fury steadily gaining momentum and then breaking beyond restraint: "Oh, that I knew where I might find him, that I might come even to his dwelling! Why don't you come out and face me like a man? Quit hiding in the remoteness of your godly position. Let the Almighty answer me!"

The creature man dares to shake his fist at the heavens, to challenge the unfairness of it all, to shout his accusations in angry defiance, to enter into conflict with God. Job's pain goes beyond that of confusion and loss. It looks into the abyss of meaningless, and Job becomes a heretic.

Becoming a heretic is a good thing that can happen to us when nothing makes sense anymore, when we desperately need answers. And to Job's credit, he sticks to his heresy in the face of enormous pressure from his friends. He is up against ultimate mystery, and, like us, he does not take kindly to what he cannot change, manage, and understand.

"Where is God in this mess?" Job questions. "Look, he passes by me, and I do not see him; he moves on, but I do not perceive him." Suppose the events of our lives amount to nothing? Suppose human history is capricious, directionless, purposeless? Suppose there is no presence within the madness that bombards us every day with feverish frequency?

"You bet your life I know about struggling uphill against the wind!" Job shouts at Therese. "You bet I do!" he shouts at God. "Where are you?"

And the silence is broken.

Maybe not in the way Job expects, but broken nonetheless. God loves Job that much. God loves us that much. But instead of answers, God has questions----that seems to be God's way. Instead of instruction, God becomes present and speaks to Job out of the whirlwind----that wind swirling around us even when we are unaware:

> Gird up your loins like a man, I will question you, and
> you shall declare to me. Where were you when I laid
> the foundation of the earth? Tell me, if you have under-

standing. Who determined its measurements—surely you know! Or who shut in the sea with doors when it burst out from the womb? Have the gates of death been revealed to you, or have you seen the gates of deep darkness? Have you comprehended the expanse of the earth? Declare, if you know all this.

"Can you run things in my stead, Job?"

Confronted with the power and presence of God, the creator and sustainer of all that is, Job repents and falls to his knees in grief and humility. The philosophical problem of suffering is not solved for him——or for us——but it now is seen within the mystery of the divine order. And that is enough. Mystery remains mystery, but it becomes mystery with meaning.

It is presumptuous to assume God cannot take anything we humans dish out, and Job's story tells us that God prefers the challenge of heresy to unthinking and unfeeling complacency. It is the defiant and confrontational Job who receives fresh vision of God, not his three friends who stick by their familiar beliefs. Correctives are available when we need them——and we will——but our danger lies in questioning too little rather than too much. After all, our questions can be the voice of God.

God is of the whirlwind: powerful, swirling around us, pushing us along, thrusting us back on ourselves, but ever present, ever with us. The voice of the wind continually calls out the invitation: "Challenge me; confront me. Shout at me if you will. Whine at me. Shake your fist at me. But I will be with you as you dare to grapple with me. And since every wind is not my voice, I will be with you on the tempestuous seas of your lives. They, too, are in my hands. It does not have to make sense. It is my way."

"The answer, my friend, is blowin' in the wind; the answer is blowin' in the wind." The "Amazing Grace" tote

was *the appropriate carrier for the sculpture, and in baptism we are granted the amazing grace to be faithful heretics. "Give us an inquiring and discerning heart," we pray, "the courage to will and to persevere, a spirit to know and to love you, and the gift of joy and wonder in all your works."*

Grant us the piercing passion of Therese and the impatience of Job. Confer the boldness to be defiant strugglers against breezes of easy answers. Give us the humble spirit of confession when we close our ears to your word. Impart a determined will to engage again and again with the whirlwind God----so we ourselves can blow through the world with confidence, love, and power.

Necessary Surprise

— Confess the faith of Christ crucified. —

SEVERAL YEARS AGO I WAS WORKING in New York City during Holy Week, and I decided to attend the Maundy Thursday service at the Church of Saint Mary the Virgin on West 46th Street right at Times Square. "Smokey Mary," they call her. I stepped from city streets into a world of dark French gothic mystery. It was like entering the cavernous belly of Jonah's whale----complete with soaring ribs. There were prayer desks and votive candles and statues. A large one of the virgin herself was up front----I believe to the right----and I remember a high pulpit hanging over the left side of the nave. What lingers now is not photographic clarity but rather ghostly fragments of impressions crowding in on each other.

The service was several hours long and beautifully choreographed: people and pieces of furniture miraculously appeared when needed. The liturgy included a symbolic footwashing, one that involved all sorts and conditions from the congregation. And the congregation included all sorts and conditions: the very young and very old, some who looked as if they lived on the streets----and likely slept on the steps of the church itself----as well as Madison Avenue executives with expensive leather briefcases. I knew they all regularly worshiped there because they all knew what to do, even when the liturgy took complicated turns.

After the communion, the rector carried the consecrated host under a special shawl in slow and solemn procession down the center aisle. Led by a backwards-walking thurifer and thick clouds of smoke, he moved under a canopy, held at its corners by four men of the congregation. I looked on in utter amazement. As the procession passed by, a wave of genuflection rolled through the nave. My knee struck the hard floor with an awkward whack.

When I finally stumbled into the chilly city night, images of the blinding blaze of the Altar of Repose, banked in startling calla-lily white, alternated with those of the stark, stripped altar and the haze of smoke encircling the lofty ceiling. I knew then that I would return to that dark cavern of mystery the next day, this time with a sense of keen anticipation. I was not disappointed.

The Good Friday service began with the singing of the Passion Chorale----"O sacred head, sore wounded"----and the first of three sermons, all of them down-to-earth and forthrightly practical, in seeming counterpoint to the rest of the liturgy. Then the priests prostrated themselves on the floor before the altar and prayed silently with the kneeling congregation. I had intended to stay for only one of the three hour-long segments of the service, but there were no segments, no breaking points. The service was three hours in duration, and no corners were cut. I didn't know when to leave, so I stayed.

John's passion story was chanted in its entirety by three male voices. The tapestry of notes floated upward and swirled around with lingering wisps of smoke from the night before. The chanting took a very long time, and the congregation stood throughout until they and the singers dropped to their knees at the point when Jesus bows his head and gives up his spirit. On the other hand, people took care of themselves. The infirm on their walkers----and they were there----inconspicuously sat and then pulled themselves up again as they needed to do so.

This day was the first time I had ever seen the Veneration of the Cross. We worshipers started in the back of the nave and then came all the way down the aisle, kneeling three times before kissing the feet of the crucified figure. We had sung three times, "Behold the wood of the Cross: whereon was hung the world's salvation." We received communion from the sacrament reserved overnight, now brought in by a deacon. The last of the three sermons was followed by the dismissal and the triumphant hymn "Diademata": "Crown him with many crowns, the Lamb upon his throne."

Somewhere in the midst of that whole Good Friday drama, the hair on my arms rose, my eyes filled with tears, and I spoke aloud, "My God, that is what happened today!" The words were not formed in my head. They emerged from way down in the womb at my center and then burst forth into my consciousness: "My God, that is what happened today." I was shaking.

I am among the fortunate. I grew up in the church and have heard the stories and sung the songs all my life. I was nearly fifty years old that Good Friday in New York; long ago I had given some kind of intellectual assent to the Good Friday/Easter event: the death and rising of God. But that year in New York in that liturgy something happened that transcended my limited capacities. I experienced Good Friday as the heart of history----the center----like the sharp point of a compass driven firmly into the earth, around which everything must turn if it is to be true to course. The fathomless truth of God's love wrapped itself around my heart and entered my loins *and issued forth in winging joy:* "My God, that is what happened!"

Somehow by God's grace on that Good Friday in New York City at the Church of Saint Mary the Virgin----Smokey Mary's----I stumbled into that realm of mystery, imagination, and surprise: the realm of the poet, the painter, the maker of music, and the child. Since that day I have come to realize that our task always is to allow for occasions----whatever and wherever they may be----in which God can sneak up on us and surprise us and over-whelm us with love. My God, this is what happens when we do!

FINALE

Home

---- *You are sealed by the Holy Spirit in Baptism
and marked as Christ's own for ever.* ----

RECENTLY I FOUND THE OPPORTUNITY to return to the
small town in rural South Georgia I had visited so many
years ago. I went straight to the house on River Street
that had been my grandmother's to see the porch and
the birdbath and the ginkgo tree, and I was not disappointed. They all were there, though the house was
smaller than the eyes of my imagination had seen.

Childhood sweethearts, the current owners had
grown up in the town. John is now the associate super-
intendent of schools. It seemed fitting to me that he is
an educator. He remembered my grandmother well, and
he remembered me. He recalled the names of forgotten
childhood playmates. Best of all, he invited me to walk
through the rooms of the house—and it all came back. I
cannot tell you how those rooms are furnished today. I
only saw them as they were over forty years ago: the
quaint settee in the sitting room, the massive oak table
in the high-ceilinged dining room, the narrow iron beds
in the sleeping rooms, and of course the green wicker
rocking chairs on the porch.

I returned to the house before leaving town the next
day. I sat alone on the porch for a while. I cried a little,
and I chuckled as I remembered. I took pictures with
my camera—probably unnecessary. I will not forget.

The walk through Nanno's house left me in a spirit of introspection, and I began to wander through the rooms of my own interior space—my home. It occurred to me that a requisite of the journey of the faithful baptized is a willingness to become friends with ourselves—the selves we all too often manage to conceal from the eye of our own scrutiny. They are, however, the ones we are to know best—the ones fashioned by the hand of God, the cherished selves God knows and intends us to be.

We hesitate, hoping to hide, but the hot eye of God sears through flimsy shields, and ash blows in the wind. The cold eye of God freezes screens of smoke, and sharp crystals shatter at our feet. God gives a holy invitation that we ignore at our peril. Not to enter is to be alienated and estranged, to wander streets alone, for we are unable to sit with others until we sit with ourselves. Intimacy will ever elude us.

Yet we are fearful. It is dangerous to become our own friend in the presence of God. It is dangerous to enter the dwelling we cohabit with the divine. The rooms through which we pass will reveal riches and possibilities beyond our imaginations. But to cross that fearsome threshold is to give consent to a life of change and the present moment's evaporating into a future of uncertainty. It is a dangerous business to choose life.

God says, "Enter." But we wrap ourselves in swirling noise so as not to hear the welcoming words. God waits.

God says, "Come in." But we entertain diversions and distractions; we seek comfort in confusion. God waits for us still.

And sometimes we cannot hear words of welcome at all, strain as we might. The door appears shut fast and bolted, and we can only knock. Then God's hand extends from within, and God gracefully wraps us in sheltering arms so we can pass through.

We climb creaking stairs to the attic of treasures. The door whines its protest to our intrusion into the dusty shrine it faithfully guards. Incense of must and mothball penetrates the air. Light filters through panes veiled by the spider priests of this sanctuary of the past, this holy of holies.

But enter we must, to throw open windows so light can flood across dusty floorboards, so breezes can rearrange cobwebs and bring fresh smells of earth and rain and brewing coffee from the kitchen below, smells of the living to raise the dead.

We open the trunk of relics. We lift out the trophies for which we sacrificed our dreams and allowed stakes to pierce our hearts. How tarnished they now seem for such a dear price. It is time to remember so we can forget. We hold up dresses of stiffened lace and flattened flower. Fragments of old melodies float from their folds and run maddeningly around in our heads. Can we weave these wisps into new music?

Out come dolls, drums, lead soldiers from battlefields of sand. Storybooks with pages tattered from turning. Yearbooks with their inscriptions of promise: "Most Likely to Succeed"; "Best Dancer." How young we were!

We find yellowed, screaming newspaper headlines that forever propelled us out of innocence, never to return. But they tell us what we must not forget, what we must tell the children, and what we must tell them to tell their children, so our remembering can become forgiving hope.

And as we move across the floorboards we bump into ghostly remains: clutter in the attic, clutter to be discarded to make room for what is to come. We are to collide with them so we can set them aside, so we can diminish their debilitating power over us. But some of these remains are more than collections of junk; some form patterns of possibility, becoming birth gifts we carry to an honored place in the main room of the house.

So we descend.

At the heart of the dwelling is the room of preparation; the place of chopping and scraping, of stirring and blending, of simmering and steaming. A place of heat and cold and of sweet smells: coffee, bread, and mysterious anticipation. The place of milk and wine and of corn and cabbage. A room for experimentation; for triumph and disaster, for learning and trying again. Perhaps a pinch of this or a dash of that would do the trick....

Shelves are to be well stocked but not filled to bursting. We are to have ingredients enough for wholesome and surprising creation but not to encourage spoilage. We are to have simple foods to nurture muscle and blood, with an occasional oyster for the soul.

This room connects us most directly with the outside world, for here we bring in that which we need for health and survival and here we prepare for others. There are those in the streets who wait with clattering plates and empty cups. There are those in neighboring houses who long for our company. We are not to be long alone in the room of preparation.

Close by is the room of light. Furniture is comfortable here. A well-stuffed chair sits near the window, a good dozing spot in the sun's warmth and a fine seat in which to settle with a book, for even on a rainy day we can see to read here.

It too is a gathering place, a place for company and conversation, for laughter and debate, for the singing of songs. On occasion we must turn down the chattering volume so we can hear and know the voice of God.

This room provides space for thought and inspiration. Bathed in warmth and sprinkled with hope, ideas grow green and vigorous. They sprout buds of freshness and issue forth cascading vines from ceiling baskets. It is a place of truth, for deception withers when doubt's murkiness is penetrated by rays of the sun. We do well to keep the windows clean.

We move to the room of rest, a place of stillness and calm. This room is down the hall and around a corner of the house. Entrance requires leaving worldly work at the door; we are to be about another sort of venture in this room, the arduous work of being and allowing. We are to be with whatever or whoever is. We are to allow invisible nourishment to seep into our cells and dreamy voices to whisper to our spirits.

This room is a place for breathing slowly and sighing deeply. Here we are released from constraints of accomplishment and effectiveness. Here our hands can be still and our minds cease whirring. We are free to draw blinds and close shutters. It is best to close the door as well. We are free to stretch our bodies full-length on the downy bed. We are free to curl up around ourselves. The colors here are the pink-grays of twilight and of dawn. Here we can know peace.

Nearby is the room of cleansing where we purge the extraneous, where we purify ourselves from toxins that pollute our relationship with God, self, and creation. This is the place where we spit out poisons of greed ingested in quests of possession and control. This is the room where we strip naked and allow streams of water to pass over us and wash us clean. This is the room where we meet our own gaze in the mirror if we dare to wipe away the steam. It can be painful to see so clearly.

There is the room of empty space, waiting to be furnished. We find it difficult to gaze upon the bare walls.

Sparsity is uncomfortable; incompleteness feels intolerable. Our temptation is to rush in and fill it with clutter, making purchases we can ill afford and buying what will not suit tomorrow's tastes or needs. Better that we go slowly. Better that we take time to wander in and out. Better that we see whom God sends to sojourn with us.

Finally, we descend another set of stairs to the basement of deep darkness. The steps are steep and twisting, and we move cautiously, running our hands along the wall as light from the hall above grows dim. We stumble on the last tread, and fingers grope for the switch that will bring relief of light, but it eludes our touch. Panic rises: maybe there is no switch! Maybe darkness is all there is to be, suffocating darkness that will shroud our proud confidence. We begin to back our way up the stairs but a touch on the elbow guides us forward. Then we seem to be alone.

We creep forward, arms extended to ward off painful collision. Every now and then we find familiar shapes in accustomed places, but mostly all is strange. Even that which we know best is alien in this realm of ghostly shadow, this abode of confusion and anxiety. Forms are blurred. Demons roam—demons who claim to have sight! Old answers do not work here, and we long for the light of certitude once at our command. We meet a chair, and we ease into its lap. Only then do we realize how our knees have been shaking.

In the basement of deep darkness we sit and wait— for what or for whom we are not sure. And as we relinquish our cravings—as we sit and wait—we become aware of another in the room. The Other. Terrifying, welcome company.

Blessed room of darkness where ordinary sight does no service. Sacred room of mystery where clarity comes from cloud. Holy room of silence where songs of eternity flood our hearing and divine darkness is the source of beaming light. As we sit and wait, deep confidence seeps into our bones. As we release our vise grip on fearful control, we touch the truth of God's intention for us. Sacred basement of deep darkness, the foundation of our dwelling.

We now can climb the stairs and continue the journey of God's holy and faithful people.

The people who walked in darkness have seen a great light; those who lived in a land of deep darkness----on them light has shined.

A Guide
for Study

by John H. Westerhoff

CALLING, OF COURSE, CAN BE READ for purely personal
enjoyment, like any other book, but it also has the possibility of becoming a resource within a variety of contexts. As a book composed of many stories it provides
its readers with both encouragement and opportunity to
reflect upon and share how their stories intersect with
God's story. Out of such storytelling Christian community emerges and we are enabled to grow in the life of
faith. What follows are a few specific suggestions for
how this book of stories might be used in concrete situations.

Retreats

A retreat is an opportunity for solitude and silence so
that one might be with God. *Calling* can help provide
an environment conducive to an engagement and conversation with God. Each day of a person's retreat can
be divided into four to six blocks of time. Each block
can begin with the retreatant reading one of the short
variations. This can be followed by time for silent meditation, concluding with a prayerful conversation with
God on the retreatant's experience during the silent
meditation. The resulting meditation experiences and
conversations with God can be recorded in a journal and
reflected upon at the close of the retreat.

Parish Quiet Days

A parish quiet day provides an opportunity for a number of people to come together for communal and personal prayer, usually around a single theme with contemplative addresses or readings to focus their meditations. For example, the day might begin with Morning Prayer and end with Evening Prayer. A possible theme would be "The Character Traits of the Baptized." In preparation, participants might read the piece "Dispositions" in *Calling*. Then during the day the variations related to "Dispositions," namely, "Danger" and "Choices," could be read aloud. After each reading a block of time for silent meditation could be provided. Then at the close of the day, before Evening Prayer, the group might gather to share their experiences during these meditations. Lunch could be eaten in silence with quiet music in the background.

Spiritual Reading

Spiritual reading is slow, reflective reading in God's presence so that God may engage us through a thought, experience, or word in the text. When that occurs we are to stop reading and enter into an engagement with God. At the close of this experience of engagement we continue our reading. Using the variation pieces, beginning with "Sunlight" and ending with "Necessary Surprise," a person can read one such piece each day alone in the morning, at the close of the day, or some other convenient time. The same can be done as an aspect of a family's devotional time each day along with prayers. In this case, a short period of silence should follow the reading. It would also be appropriate for the persons gathered to discuss the reading.

Vestry Meetings

Few vestries set aside time for learning as part of their meetings, but *Calling* provides a resource for correcting this neglect. All the essays under the second movement, "Baptism and Community," along with the theme "Creativity and Conflict" under the third movement, can become useful resources for study and discussion. They can be read individually before or corporately during the meeting. The questions for discussion might be: "What insights are there in this essay for our parish? What are the implications of these insights? And how can we address these implications?"

Mission/Long Range Planning Committees

The essays under the third movement, "Baptism and Responsibility," can enhance and enliven the work of such groups. Discussion questions similar to those suggested for vestry meetings might be helpful.

Vocational Discernment Groups

The first movement, "Baptism and Ministry," can be helpful to those who are striving to discern what God would like them to do with their lives. In the case of those who are considering ordination or some form of professional lay ministry within the church, the questions for discussion need to focus particularly on the participants' understanding of ministry. This same movement also can be useful as a discussion starter with vocational groups of business people, nurses, doctors, lawyers, teachers, salespeople, laborers, secretaries, farmers, and so forth who want to consider how their daily lives and vocations can be used as contexts for ministry, for serving God by doing God's will.

Baptismal/Confirmation Preparation

Both the first movement, "Baptism and Ministry," and the third, "Baptism and Responsibility," can be read and discussed by adults preparing for baptism, by parents and godparents preparing for the baptism of a child, and by older adolescents and adults preparing for confirmation. The questions ought to focus on the meaning of baptism and the life the baptized are called to live. Note that each piece in *Calling* is headed with words from the baptismal liturgy in the Episcopal Church's Book of Common Prayer. These readings from *Calling* might be used when that section of the rite is discussed. Another possibility is that the person responsible for the preparation of these candidates might use these pieces for personal inspiration.

Lenten Study Book

A five-week study for groups can be developed out of the prelude, "Calling"; the themes "Holy Habits," "Dispositions," and "Covenant" under the first movement; and the finale, "Home." Individuals can read these same pieces for inspiration. If used in a study group, the question might be: "What questions does this piece raise for you?" When all the participants' questions are stated, they can become the basis for discussion.

Adult Education Class

This book can easily become a semester or twelve-week course, using the movements and themes for the twelve sessions. Although it would be preferable for the sections to be read before class, they are brief enough to be read quietly at the beginning of a class session. Questions that might be raised include: "What did you read that was of particular interest to you? What was your reaction, including your feelings about it? As you reflect on your reaction, what insights are there for you? What can you learn from your reaction? Reflecting on your insights, what are their implications for your life?"

Bible Study

Throughout the book there are reflections on Scripture. Some examples follow: Under the movement "Baptism and Ministry," see: "Sunlight," Matthew 8:27-38; "All the Baptized," Mark 10:35-45; "Danger," Matthew 15:21-28; "Choices," Luke 4:1-13; and "Broken Promises," Joshua 24:1-2a, 14-25.

Under the movement "Baptism and Community," see: "Bones," Ezekiel 37:1-14; "Wings," Matthew 9:35–10:15; "Illumination," 1 Kings 19:9-18 and Mark 9:2-29.

And under the movement "Baptism and Responsibility," see: "Royal People," 1 Peter 2:4-10; "Confrontation," John 2:13-22; and "Heresy," Job 38:1-11, 16-18.

First read the passage from Scripture and have each person write it in their own words. Then have each person, in silence, enter into the text and experience it personally. Next, read aloud the appropriate piece from *Calling* and invite everyone to compare and contrast their experience and learnings with those of the author and of the others in the study group.

Church School Teacher Training

In church school teacher training we often neglect both the spirituality of teaching and the spiritual life of the teacher. The prelude, "Calling," can help address the first and the finale, "Home," the second. It would be best if these readings were dealt with spiritually so as to increase the possibility for learning.

In the spirituality of teaching sessions, read "Calling" slowly. Then provide time for silence and ask people to review their lives until they discover someone that was important for their learning. Then give everyone an opportunity to tell their stories. At the end, focus on the character traits that made these persons important for their learning and growth.

Before they read "Home" in the spiritual life of the teacher sessions, suggest that they close their eyes and consider the piece to be read as a directed meditation intended to take them into their interior life. Read the piece slowly and after each room is described let there be silence so people can go inside that same room in their interior life. At the close, give everyone an opportunity to share their experiences, what they learned, and what implications that learning might have for their spiritual lives.

These might also be used with a parents group or a combined parents and teachers group.